ESSAYS

SELENA STEWART-ALEXANDER | PATRICE K. JOHNSON | CAITLIN S. STANFORD

EASTFIELD COLLEGE

THINK
Write!

Kendall Hunt
publishing company

Kendall Hunt
publishing company

www.kendallhunt.com
Send all inquiries to:
4050 Westmark Drive
Dubuque, IA 52004-1840

Dedication

I would like to dedicate this book to all of the students whom I have been fortunate enough to teach over the years. I am honored to have been a part of their lives, I am humbled by their struggles, and I am inspired by their resilience. In addition, I would like to dedicate this book to my husband, Brian; our son, Malik; my parents, Oscar, my late mother Murriel, and my stepmother Liz; my sisters by birth, my late sister Ida, Linda, and Michelle; and my sisters by choice, Kendra and Darlene. Special thanks to my coauthors for embracing this idea of putting down on paper what we do in the classroom.

—Selena

I would like to dedicate this book to my late mother, Mary D. Franklin, who served in the education field for nearly 40 years trying to ensure that students were college ready; to my late father, Verse Franklin, who always said I had a book inside me; to my wonderful family, Kevin, Kenasia, Tyson, and Mari, who allowed me to work on this project and provided me with undying support; to my "other" mom, Leslie Robinson, who encouraged me during my early adult years to aim for the stars and to become successful; and to my coauthors who encouraged me to render my best work; and finally, to all of my students who have inspired me over the years.

—Patrice

I would like to dedicate this book to my husband, Stephen; my parents, Kerry and Karen; my grandmother, Billie Osborn; and my late grandmother, Theeopal Stanford. Additionally, I want to dedicate this book to my coauthors, without whom this project would not have been possible. Special thanks to Dorothy Bennett for her fabulous student essays, Jane Stanford for teaching me the "who vs. whom" trick, Deborah Chester, and Mrs. Pape, my first grade teacher who encouraged me to write books. Finally, I would like to dedicate this book to all my students, past, present, and future.

—Caitlin

Contents

PART I

The Writing Process and Basic Essay Format

INTRODUCTION TO THE WRITING PROCESS

Writing can be an intimidating task, especially if you have not had to write anything in several years, your job does not require you to communicate through writing, or if you do not know the basic skills regarding the writing process. Many times, you may become frustrated because you cannot get your thoughts onto paper. This chapter deals specifically with thought processes and strategies that enable you to achieve success before and while writing sentences, paragraphs, and essays.

The writing process consists of four steps: prewriting, drafting, revising, and editing. The following chapters go over each step in detail so that you have a clear understanding of each. Below is an overview of each step.

Step 1: Prewriting
Successful writers know that it is important to not just jump into writing about a topic, but to take some time and think and plan what you want to say.

Step 2: Drafting
After getting your thoughts down in the prewriting stage, it is time to organize them and write your first draft, knowing that perfection is not the goal at this time.

Step 3: Revising
During the revising step, you review what you have written during the drafting step and move things around, take information out, and add more details. The revising stage focuses on checking your organization and content and the clarity of your message.

Step 4: Editing
Editing is the final step in the writing process, where you check for mechanical errors, like spelling, punctuation, and grammar mistakes. Too many of these errors will cause your readers to become distracted from your message and cause you to lose credibility as a writer.

Chapter 1

Prewriting

Key Terms

Prewriting, meta-cognition, audience, purpose, free writing, listing, clustering, asking questions, outlining, building a pyramid

Prewriting Process

As a student writer, you may use the terms prewriting process and writing process synonymously, meaning you lump both of these processes into one process and act as though they mean the same thing. Although these processes are closely related, it is important to realize that one comes before the other. The Latin prefix "pre-" means **before**. Add this Latin prefix to the word "writing" and you have the term **prewriting**, which ultimately means **before writing**. This is also the first of the two processes mentioned above. It is important for you to realize that something must be done before a sentence can become part of a paragraph or a paragraph can become part of an essay. Therefore, the question is **what must be done before you write an essay?** A major part of the prewriting process has to do with the way you think about the topic for which you are being asked to write.

A term that captures this ultimate thought process is called "**meta-cognition**" or thinking about thinking. Be aware that the way you approach both the prewriting and the writing processes will determine how successful you are in classes that require thoughtful writing assignments. Meta-cognition has to be practiced in order to be mastered. Thinking about how you think is important because it directly affects how you respond to writing topics. This improvement in thinking should take place long before you get to the college campus or boot up your computer if you are taking an online or distance learning class. Remember, you may be a student who has not written in several semesters or years or you may just not like writing at all. It is important to change your attitude about prewriting and writing from negative to positive.

THINK *Write!*

Activity 1.1 Meta-cognition

Look at the following topics and think of all the words that come to mind about that topic. Do not write them down . . . just THINK!

1. Vacations
2. Going green
3. Abortion
4. Colleges and universities
5. Health insurance

Once you have practiced thinking, it is time to write or type some of your ideas. The main function for generating ideas revolves around thinking and sorting your thoughts. When you run out of thoughts, question your thinking. Know that all of your thoughts will not be relevant to the topic you are writing about, but during the prewriting process, random thoughts are permitted. There will be time to sort and organize these thoughts later. If you think about thinking often and correctly, generating ideas about a topic may become an easier and more enjoyable task.

Audience and Purpose

Before you start getting ideas down on paper, you need to think about two important factors. One is your **audience**. Audience is who you are writing for, your reader. Audience is important because it determines how you will write—word choice and tone. If you are writing for a friend, you might use a conversational tone and slang words. However, if you are writing for your professor, a more formal, academic tone is needed in standard American English.

Purpose is your reason for writing. There are three main purposes when you write: to inform, to persuade, or to entertain. It is possible for the purpose to overlap, but keeping your purpose in mind will help you stay on track. Oftentimes, purpose is determined by your mode of writing. If you are writing a descriptive essay, for example, your purpose is to entertain by creating a vivid picture in your reader's mind. The argument essay, however, is meant to persuade the reader as you defend your position on an issue.

Prewriting Strategies

There are several strategies you can use to generate ideas: **free writing, listing, clustering, asking questions, outlining**, and **building a pyramid**.

Free Writing

Write freely about whatever comes to your mind about a topic. At this point, you are not worried about errors in grammar, spelling, mechanics, or formatting. At first glance, free writing may look like a paragraph or essay, but when you begin to revise and edit, you will find there is much correction needed to enhance the final draft. This strategy is popular because you are "free" and less apprehensive about writing.

FREE WRITING EXAMPLE

Topic: soccer

I have played soccer my whole life. I started when I was 5. When I was little. We just chased the ball around the field crazy style. When I was older I learned positions. I started out as a halfback. Then forward for years. Now I play wheerever needed. Sometimes that's defence. Soccer also maens the world cup. That's fun to watch. U stay up all night. I cheer for the US and Germany. AWESOME!

 THINK

Activity 1.2 Free Writing

Try free writing about one of the following topics. Do not worry about grammar, punctuation, or spelling.

1. Family planning
2. Diet
3. Emotions
4. Sports

Listing

When you use this strategy, you write the topic at the top of the page and then write one word or a small phrase per line about the topic. This is usually a vertical list down the margin of a piece of paper or computer screen. This list is similar to a grocery store list. You know that there are several reasons for writing a grocery list. First, you are writing down items that you want or need (necessity). Secondly, you may write the list to keep you organized so you do not over spend on items that you do not need (irrelevance). Therefore, like grocery shopping, you create a list so that when you begin drafting, you use only the ideas you need and eliminate irrelevant ideas.

LISTING EXAMPLE

Topic: places to sightsee in Europe

Paris

Eiffel Tower

The Louvre

Leaning Tower of Pisa

German castles

Belgian chocolate

Anne Frank's house

Vienna

Paris Opera House

Old Greek ruins

Vatican

Trevi Fountain

THINK *Write!*

Activity 1.3 Listing

Try listing about one of the following topics. Do not worry about spelling, punctuation, or grammar.

1. Fast food
2. Scary moments
3. Places tourists should visit in your city
4. Pets some people consider dangerous

A SUPER LIST

Try this: Write a normal list. Then, using the numbers one, two, and three, go back and number the relevant ideas about your topic. For every idea that has a one beside it, you can assume those ideas will go into body paragraph one. Likewise, every item that has a two beside it will go into body paragraph two and so on. The items in the list that do not have a number by them will most likely not be included in your essay. Remember, once you get to the revising stage of the writing process you may choose to organize your work differently in order to maintain coherency throughout the essay. This only means that what you thought body paragraph number one would be about has shifted to either body paragraphs two or three.

Review the example below. Notice that the writer plans to discuss different aspects of dogs regarding food, breed, and training. Notice how the writer categorizes the relationships using 1, 2, and 3. Finally, notice how anything that is irrelevant to the three aspects is crossed out.

Dogs

1 Food	~~Vicious~~
~~Hairy~~	2 Maltese
~~Friendly~~	3 Training
2 Breeds	3 Kennel training
1 Alpo	2 Poodle
1 Science Diet	~~Cat~~
~~Mean~~	3 Leash training

Clustering

To create a cluster, you actually draw a circle in the middle of a piece of paper and write the topic in the circle. Like free writing, you then branch out from the "topic circle" and write whatever comes to your mind about the topic. If necessary, you may even branch out from your "subtopics" for more ideas. The cluster provides you with a visual picture of ideas and possible organization. No matter how small or large the cluster may be, ideas are indeed being generated. Remember, during the prewriting process, there are no errors being generated, only ideas. You may find that what you thought was irrelevant may prove to be valuable when you begin to add supporting details to your essay. You are encouraged to jump right in and continue *thinking!*

CLUSTERING EXAMPLE

Topic: social media

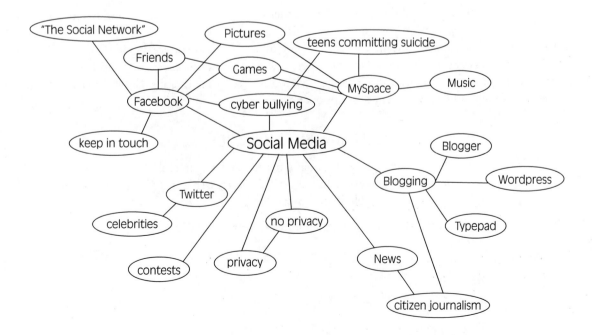

THINK *Write!*

Activity 1.4 Clustering

Try clustering about one of the following topics. Do not worry about grammar, punctuation, or spelling.

1. Gossip
2. Random drug testing
3. Community service requirement
4. Hip Hop culture

Asking Questions

Asking questions includes two steps. The first step is writing questions about a topic on a piece of paper or computer screen. After you have asked who, what, when, where, and why about the topic, then you go back and complete the second step, which is answering as many questions as you can. The rationale behind asking questions is that you are actually generating ideas and support for your essay. Like free writing, clustering, and listing, asking questions will get you closer to the ideas you need to write an essay. Review the questions about dogs below.

ASKING QUESTIONS EXAMPLE

Who breeds dogs?

What types of food do dogs like to eat?

When are dogs ready to be trained?

Where should dogs go to be trained?

Why are there so many crossbreeds of dogs?

How do people decide what to feed dogs?

Outlining

An **outline** is a written chart outlining your ideas in order of importance. Numbers and letters are used to distinguish your main topics from your subtopics. Outlines provide you with a "shell" of the essay you will write. Once the shell is created, you fill it in with a controlling idea and supporting ideas that will eventually turn into your essay. Like the super list, the order in which you write the essay is ultimately up to you. Remember, the outline can be used interchangeably to write body paragraphs. Simply change the thesis statement to a topic sentence, and fill in the supporting details.

OUTLINING EXAMPLE

Thesis Statement: Playing video games has many negative effects on children and teens because the games are full of graphic images, they are distracting, and they can increase the likelihood of a child becoming obese.

I.   First, video games are full of graphic images. (topic sentence for body paragraph 1)
   a.   Violence/murder
   b.   Blood
   c.   Sexual content

    II. Next, video games can distract children and teens from responsibilities. (topic sentence for body paragraph 2)

        a. School

        b. Chores

        c. Friends/face-to-face interaction

   III. Lastly, video games can cause children and teens to become obese. (topic sentence for body paragraph 3)

        a. Sitting too much

        b. Never go outside

        c. Problems associated with obesity

Conclusion: Video games have many negative effects on children and teens. They are very graphic. They are also distractions. Additionally, they can lead to obesity.

THINK *Write!*

Activity 1.5 Outlining

Try creating an outline answering the following question: Where are three places you would love to take a vacation?

Thesis Statement: _____

_____

Topic Sentence Body Paragraph 1

I. _____

    a. _____

    b. _____

    c. _____

Topic Sentence Body Paragraph 2

II. _____

    a. _____

    b. _____

    c. _____

Topic Sentence Body Paragraph 3

III. _____

    a. _____

    b. _____

    c. _____

Conclusion: _____

_____

_____

Building a Pyramid

A pyramid is another prewriting option. It is similar to an outline but is also a graphic organizer to help you sort ideas and support for your essay. A pyramid has four sections. The top of the pyramid contains the topic and the controlling idea from the thesis statement. It is a single box. The upper middle section of the pyramid has three boxes that will contain the three points of your thesis statement. The lower middle section is for the supports. It has three boxes that are divided up into three or more sections. Support for your three main reasons should be written in the three boxes. The base of the pyramid will serve as the conclusion. The objective when filling in the pyramid is to gain as many supporting details as you can in order to complete the essay.

Playing video games has many negative effects on children and teens because . . .		
they are full of graphic images,	they are distracting,	and they can increase the likelihood of a child becoming obese.
many games are full of violence and killing people	distract from school; child's grades can slip	too much time sitting can make one obese
some of the violence is very graphic and bloody	distract from doing household chores	childhood obesity is becoming a problem for U.S.
some video games have sexual content as well	distract from living real life and interacting face to face	obesity can lead to health issues, like heart problems and diabetes

Video games have many negative effects on children. They are too violent for children to play. The games also distract children from responsibilities. Additionally, they can increase the likelihood of childhood obesity.

2

Chapter

Drafting

© colia, 2012. Used under license from Shutterstock, Inc.

Key Terms

Drafting, thesis statement, topic, controlling idea, three main points, parallel structure, introduction, body paragraphs, topic sentence, conclusion

Now that you have practiced the art of thinking during the prewriting process, it is time to put this practice to work regarding the actual writing process. The steps to this process do not necessarily have to be in the order they are listed below. However, as you learn to master this process, it may help you more if you follow the steps of the writing process.

Drafting

By now you most certainly have been assigned a topic, or you have been directed to generate your own essay topic. You have the most valuable pieces of information: a topic and prewriting. Never throughout the prewriting or writing processes are you allowed to stop thinking. Thinking critically about ideas and about your topic must continue from start to finish. When you have reviewed all of your ideas, it is time to start writing. The words **drafting** and writing will be used interchangeably throughout this book. These two words have the same meaning. At this point, you are beginning to pay attention to the rules of writing regarding formatting and length. Your instructor will specify all expectations regarding the essay.

The drafting stage of the writing process can be encompassed in three steps: writing a thesis statement, organizing ideas, and writing your rough draft.

As you decide how the ideas you generated will be incorporated into the essay, it is important that you come up with a **thesis statement**. A thesis statement is one sentence that will explain to the reader what the essay will be about. This statement will contain a main idea and three or more supporting points or reasons. Typically, the thesis statement can be written or implied. Placement of the thesis statement can differ. For example, you could place it at the beginning of the introduction, or you could make it the last sentence in the introduction paragraph. More than likely, your professor may ask you to place the thesis statement at the end of the introduction paragraph, making it the last sentence. Until you become a more sophisticated writer, placing the thesis statement at the end of the introduction will help you and your reader easily know how the rest of your essay will be organized.

Thesis statements generally have three parts, although not always.

Topic: What you are writing about or the main idea of your essay.

Controlling idea: What you are saying about the topic; the controlling idea "controls" the rest of the essay. Everything will relate back to it.

Three main points: What will be covered in each of your three body paragraphs/your three main reasons to support the topic and controlling idea.

Below is an example of a thesis statement.

| topic | | controlling idea | main point 1 | main point 3 |

Dogs are considered to be man's best friend because dogs are loyal, kind, and smart.

| | main point 2 | |

The topic, or main idea, is "dogs." The controlling idea is that they are considered to be "man's best friend." Therefore, the rest of the essay will be about the good points of dogs because it "controls" the essay. No bad points about dogs will be mentioned. The three main points, or three main reasons, are *loyal*, *kind*, and *smart*. Every essay must contain a sentence like this.

THINK *Write!*

Activity 2.1 Identifying Thesis Statement Parts

Circle the topic in the following thesis statements. Then, underline the controlling idea. Finally, number the three main points 1, 2, and 3.

1. Three countries I would like to travel to are Russia, France, and Greece.
2. Playing video games has many negative effects on children and teens because the games are full of graphic images, they are distracting, and they can increase the likelihood of a child becoming obese.
3. The *Lord of the Rings* films are the best movies ever made because of the actors, the special effects, and the setting.

THINK *Write!*

Activity 2.2 Finishing Thesis Statements

The thesis statements below are missing one main point. Finish the thesis statements by creating the final point for each.

1. Tigers would not make good house pets because they are dangerous, they cost too much, and they _____ .
2. Social networking is a fabulous invention because it allows people to keep in contact, share pictures, and _____
3. If I won the lottery, I would buy a new house, travel around the world, and _____
_____ .

As you begin to think about how to mold your ideas into a thesis statement, it is very important to write a thesis statement that possesses **parallel structure**. Parallel structure refers to similarity in words and phrases. It means that all items in a list are "balanced" or "match" in regard to parts of speech. In other words, all items in a list contain −ing words, to + a verb, verbs, nouns, adjectives, adjectives + nouns, or phrases.

If you reexamine the thesis statement previously discussed about dogs, you will see an example of correct parallel structure.

Dogs are considered to be man's best friend because dogs are *loyal, kind, and smart.*

Notice the words *loyal, kind,* and *smart.* They are all singular adjectives to describe the qualities of dogs. The words follow an a, b, c pattern. If the writer chooses, however, to change the words to phrases, then all of the words must be changed. Look at the following thesis statement below about dogs. This time the writer decided to write phrases to describe the qualities of dogs, which means the writer is using the aaa, bbb, ccc pattern.

Dogs are considered to be man's best friend because *they are loyal pets, they are naturally kind,* and *they are usually smart.*

Whatever thesis statement you choose to incorporate into your essay, it should match one of these patterns so that it flows easily when read aloud. It is not correct to mix the two patterns into one thesis statement as doing so will yield an unparallel structure that is choppy when read aloud.

THINK *Write!*

Activity 2.3 Parallel Structure

Below are five thesis statements that are not parallel. Make corrections to the parallelism.

1. My favorite morning activities include walking, to jog, and swimming.
2. To release my stress, I play video games, listen to music, and watching television.
3. Horror movies are scary because there are psycho killers, have gory scenes, and there is suspense.
4. Community colleges should be a student's first choice because they are inexpensive, they offer a quality education, and close to home.
5. Recycling is important because it saves resources, it keeps landfills from overflowing, and animals' habitat.

THINK *Write!*

Activity 2.4 Parallel Structure

Choose three of the topics below and write a thesis statement that has a main topic, an idea about the topic, and three reasons. Try to use one of the patterns discussed above (a, b, c OR aaa, bbb, ccc). Remember not to mix the two patterns.

Example: Topic—Cats

a, b, c, structure: *Cats make good pets because they are easy, amusing, and cuddly.*

aaa, bbb, ccc structure: *Cats make good pets because they are easy to take care of, they are amusing to play with, and they are fun to cuddle.*

1. Parades
2. Fast food restaurants
3. Blogging
4. Mission work
5. Airplanes

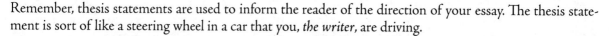

Remember, thesis statements are used to inform the reader of the direction of your essay. The thesis statement is sort of like a steering wheel in a car that you, *the writer*, are driving.

Recall that the thesis statement is a part of the **introduction paragraph.** The introduction is the first paragraph in the essay. It has three purposes: to introduce the topic, to catch the reader's interest, and to present the thesis statement, or main idea, of the essay. Introductions are covered in depth in Chapter 4.

The body paragraphs follow the introduction. The body can consist of as many paragraphs as necessary to express your ideas, but for a traditional five-paragraph essay, there are three body paragraphs. Each body paragraph requires a strong, clear **topic sentence**. The topic sentence is the first sentence of each body paragraph, and primarily, it tells the reader what the paragraph will be about. The topics of the body paragraphs will come from the thesis statement; therefore, each body paragraph should reference one of the three main points in the thesis. For example, using the first example thesis statement about dogs, topic sentence number one will discuss how dogs are loyal, topic sentence number two will discuss how dogs are kind, and topic sentence number three will discuss how dogs are smart. Once you have written your topic sentences you must support them with details that relate to the thesis statement. Both body paragraphs and topic sentences are covered further in Chapter 5.

THINK *Write!*

Activity 2.5

Below are two examples of essay outlines. Fill in the missing information for the following outlines.

1. Thesis Statement: Smoking in public restaurants should be banned because it poses health risks, it smells, and _____ .

   Topic Sentence #1: One reason smoking should be banned is that it poses health risks.

   Topic Sentence #2: Another reason smoking should be banned in restaurants is that cigarette smoke smells.

   Topic Sentence #3: The third reason people should not be allowed to smoke in restaurants is that _____ .

2. Thesis Statement: The day we spent at Six Flags will be a day I will never forget because of the park rides, the entertainment, and the food.

   Topic Sentence #1: First of all, the park rides at Six Flags are extremely exciting.

   Topic Sentence #2: Secondly, the _____ is awesome.

   Topic Sentence #3: _____ .

The last paragraph in the essay is the **conclusion**. The purpose of the conclusion is to sum up your main points and give the reader a sense of closure. Conclusions are covered more in Chapter 6.

The Traditional Five-Paragraph Essay Layout

Title (the first glimpse of what the essay will be about)

Introduction

- ✏ Attention Getter and/or background information about the topic

- ✏ Thesis Statement: states the main idea of the essay; three points are included

Body Paragraph One

Topic Sentence #1: states the essay's first point (Thesis Point #1)

Support:

Concluding Sentence:

Body Paragraph Two

Topic Sentence #2: states the essay's second point (Thesis Point #2)

Support:

Concluding Sentence:

Body Paragraph Three

Topic Sentence #3: states the essay's third point (Thesis Point #3)

Support:

Concluding Sentence:

Conclusion Paragraph

Summarizes the essay, restates the thesis, and brings the essay to an end

SAMPLE ESSAY
Wondrous Dogs ^{title}

Dogs have been around for centuries. They are one of the first animals domesticated and thought of as family pets. In ancient times, dogs have been known to be thought of as royalty in some cultures. Different breeds have been used for different tasks that have proven to be very helpful to humans. It has often been thought that dogs act the way they were trained; dogs can be ferocious and aggressive, or they can be docile and mild mannered. Dogs are considered to be man's best friend because they are loyal, kind, and smart. [thesis statement]

[topic sentence 1]
First, dogs have a tendency to be extremely loyal. Because initially dogs, like other animals, ran in packs, it is thought that their ability to be loyal is innate. For example, dogs, like humans, can feel a sense of love and compassion, and in return, they become loyal to those who show them a caring attitude. Often times even if a dog is mistreated, it will still be loyal to whom it believes is its family. Dogs love companionship, and they will be loyal to those who are closest to them.

[topic sentence 2]
Secondly, dogs have been known to be one of the kindest creatures on earth. Some dog breeds are so kind they are used to aid disabled humans by guiding them and protecting them during their day to day activities. For example, in America, as well as abroad, there are dogs used specifically as seeing-eye dogs, fire dogs, and search and rescue dogs. These types of dogs have an innate ability to care for humans who cannot defend or care for themselves. Other types of dogs are naturally kind, as well. Unlike some animals, dogs can sense when their masters are scared, sad, and angry. Because of their kindness, they make great companions for children as well as the elderly.

[topic sentence 3]
Lastly, dogs have been known to be extremely smart. The type of breed determines the dog's level of intelligence. For example, the Border collie is considered one of the smartest dogs. This breed has an innate ability to herd such animals as sheep, goats, and cows. The German shepherd is known to be intelligent and is often used to assist police officers with the daily task of protecting the community. The Labrador retriever is also smart and is used to aid the seeing and hearing impaired. These particular breeds are known to be some of the smartest dogs.

[thesis restatement]
Dogs are wonderful animals. They are loyal to their owners. In addition, dogs are very kind. Dogs are also extremely smart; some breeds are smarter than others. Because of the innate ability they possess to care, serve, and protect, dogs make great companions for human beings.

Marginal labels: introduction, body paragraph 1, body paragraph 2, body paragraph 3, conclusion

THINK *Write!* **Review Questions**

1. True/False   Drafting and writing are not interchangeable terms.

2. True/False   Every essay has a thesis statement, whether implied or stated.

3. True/False   Parallel structure can sometimes be ignored in a thesis statement.

4. True/False   The thesis statement states the main idea of the essay and determines the direction of the essay.

5. True/False   The traditional essay consists of five paragraphs.

Revising and Editing

Key Terms

Revising, unity, support, coherence, transitional devices, titles, editing, publishing

Once you have written your first draft it is time to **revise** for unity, support, coherence, and sentence exploration. As during the prewriting process, thought processes must place you directly into a framework so that you understand the necessity for improvement and change. When revising and editing, you consciously think about how to make what you are trying to convey clearer. It is now time to care about details and support; it is also time to consider spelling and mechanics. Notice that you have generated many ideas up to this point and you have somewhat of a plan for development; however, if you believe your essay is indeed well written, it is still important when revising to cover the important bases or foundations of the writing process to ensure meaning is being conveyed to your reader. Below are some standard essay writing bases that must be covered before the final draft is submitted or published.

Unity

Unity refers to the essay having clear topics in which you adhere to throughout the entire essay. This means that once you have determined what topic and reasons you will write about, you must stick to them and never venture off the path allowing new topics or reasons to infiltrate your essay. Once you have established unity in your essay, you are on a clear path to conveying understanding to the reader.

For example, if the thesis statement declares that the essay will be about how dogs are loyal, kind, and smart, it is not appropriate to address how monkeys climb trees at the zoo. As a writer, you must stay on topic and focused.

Support

Support refers to providing the reader adequate and specific details. Adequate support means that you have provided the reader with enough details. Specific support means you include relevant details about the topic as opposed to irrelevant details.

For example, if you were asked to narrate or tell a story about a car accident you witnessed, you would most likely include details about the color of the vehicle in question or the impact of the vehicle that caused the accident. As a witness, you would most likely leave out information about an airplane that was flying overhead when the accident occurred unless the airplane was involved in the accident. It may be true that the airplane flew overhead; however, it is not relevant to the accident and should be omitted.

Coherence

Coherence refers to organizing ideas in a logical, consistent, and parallel manner so that the reader understands what you are trying to convey. During the prewriting process, as the brain starts to generate ideas about the topic, you are most likely thinking about what details to include or omit. You begin to answer questions about the order of your ideas and how you will list them in the thesis or what support you will include in the body of the essay. Questions like these are characteristics of coherence, which determine the direction of the essay. After you have been given an essay topic, it is important to think about the topic and come up with at least three ideas that relate directly to that topic. Once you have come up with ideas, it is important to place them strategically in the essay in order to provide the reader with the most clarity.

For example, in the essay "Wondrous Dogs," the writer had to decide the order of the three points: dogs are loyal, kind, and smart. The writer began with thought processes that eventually determined the order of the points. As you strengthen the coherency in your essay, you may find that your initial ideas change several times from start to finish.

Transitional Devices

Transitional devices, or transitions, will help you create coherency in your essay. Transitions help you move smoothly from one idea to another, whether it is from paragraph to paragraph or from idea to idea inside a paragraph. Below is a chart to help you remember and correctly use transitional devices. You may notice that some transitional devices can be used in more than one way.

Space transitions **show direction or location**.	In front, in front of, behind, next to, beside, above, around, between, by, down, in, near, on, over, toward, under, to the right, to the left
Time (chronological) transitions **show the order in which events occur(ed)**.	First, next, before, after, then, as, during, immediately, later, meanwhile, now, often, previously, suddenly, when, while, second, third, last, finally
Addition transitions **show additional ideas**.	Also, next, furthermore, another, finally, first, in addition, as well
Cause and effect transitions **show the effect of something**.	Therefore, as a result, as a consequence of, because, since, consequently, so, thus, ultimately, in conclusion
Contrast transitions signal **contrasting or differing ideas**.	However, although, even though, nevertheless, on the other hand, but, in spite of, in contrast, instead, yet
Example transitions **help to show examples or illustrate ideas better**.	For example, for instance, including, such as, like

With coherence as well as unity and support, understanding the function of each base will eventually yield your best writing.

Unity, support, and coherence are closely related. Biologically, brothers and sisters are more closely related than two cousins. Therefore, unity, support, and coherence are so closely related they are like brothers and sisters. You cannot omit one base and think the standards for the other bases will be met efficiently.

Titles

Whether you add a title as you draft your essay or wait until you revise, **titles** are an important part of the essay. They have two purposes: they let the reader know in a nutshell what your essay will be about, and they assist the reader in wanting to read your essay. Below are some title tips.

Title Tips

- Center your title.
- Keep your title short; it should be a few words or a short phrase of four to six words at the most.
- Make certain your title is NOT a complete sentence.
- Do not bold, enlarge, or put a period at the end of titles.
- Do not italicize, underline, or use quotation marks in the title of your own paper.
- Do not use the prompt question as your title: What are three places you would like to visit?

  ✂ Capitalize only certain letters of words in your title: the first letter of the first word, only the first letter of major words in the middle, and the first letter of the last word.

  ✂ Try to be creative with your title.

Here are some examples of titles. Pay close attention to what letters are capitalized and that none of the titles are complete sentences.

Winning the Lottery: A Life Changing Event

My Stress Busters

College Survival Tactics 101

Stubbing out Cigarettes once and for All

THINK *Write!*

Activity 3.1

Create a title for an essay about the following:

1. Dating tips
2. The worst job you ever had
3. The death penalty
4. Social media
5. A time you experienced injustice

Editing

Once you have thought about the topic, organized your ideas, written your first draft, revised the essay, and added a title if you have not previously done so, it is now time to make your essay shine. To do this, you must study and learn the process of **editing**. When you edit your work, you do so to ensure there are no errors in your essay. You must edit carefully because you want to submit an essay that exhibits mastery of the learning outcomes for that particular essay. When you edit, there are several factors to consider: grammar, punctuation, mechanics, spelling, and formatting.

THINK *Write!*

Activity 3.2

The essay below needs to be revised and edited. Check the essay for coherence. Do you feel enough transitional devices were used to easily follow the writer's ideas? Check for support. Do you feel the writer adequately supported the thesis statement? Check for unity. Do you feel the writer stayed on topic? Finally, check for errors in spelling, grammar, punctuation, mechanics, and formatting. See Rules of Writing: The Sweet Sixteen.

Places I have seen.

Traveling is very fun. It's nice to see new places and new things. I have enjoyed visiting three places; Denali, Ocho Rios, and New Orleans, LA.

First, Denali which is in Alaska, is a fun place to visit. It has mountains . They are beautiful, and have snow on them year roung. Mt. McKinley is in Denali National Park and it is the tallest mountain in the United states. The highlight of my trip was taking a plane ride around Mt. McKinley's peak. I visited De Nali in the summer time. It seemed like the sun never set, and even at four in the morning it was sunny in my window, which allowed us to do alot of outdoor activities. In the state park, we hiked and mountain climbed. We also so a black bear and some mountain goats. I would recommend every visit Denali, Alaska, at least once.

Another places I have enjoyed visiting is New Orleans, LA. I love the architecture their. I like to go to the Garden District and see the big mansions. Some were built over 100 yrs ago. Another reason I love New Orleans is because of the atmosphere in thre French Quarter. It's so exciting to see a jazz band jamming on a street corner. You can just sit and listen to them all day. Of course, it's also fun to go to Bourbon Street and have a hurricane or hand grenade. These are both drinks. Just don't have too many! Haha. Furthermore, New Orleans has strange above ground cemetaries. St. Louis Number 1 in the French Quarter is where Marie Laveau, the Voodoo Queen of New Orleans, is buried. People leave offerings to her in front of her grave so that her spirit might do some voodoo work for them!!!!!! Last time I was there, people had left Mardi Gras beads glasses of water roses, and other things. People also mark X's all over the grave .It's weird but interesting. New Orleans is always a lot of fun.

I visited Ocho Rios, Jamaica twice. First, I went to Jimmy Buffet's Margaritaville restaurant and had some Jerk Chicken. Later I rode a zip line down a mountain. At one point, the guides let me freefall down a 50 foot drop. I screamed like a banshee. I also climbed Dunn's River Falls. The water was so cold! Everyone had to hold hands because the rocks were slippery. Jamaica was very beautiful, but also humid. The beaches were nice too I swam a lot and snorkeled a small reef.

Traveling is interesting, I had some places I really liked visiting. I loved Denali, Ocho Rios, and New Orleans. Everyone should travell

---

Publishing

After you are finished prewriting, drafting, revising, and editing, it is now time to publish your work. **Publishing** means you are ready to turn in your essay to your professor because you are confident that all parts of the prewriting process and the writing process have been followed closely. When you publish your essays consistently and correctly, it gives you a boost of confidence and encouragement regarding the writing process. Submitting well written essays gives you a positive feeling toward your work and signifies an end to another journey through the writing process.

THINK *Write!* Review Questions

1. Why is unity important?

2. Why do you need adequate support in your essay?

3. What does coherence mean to your reader?

4. Give two examples of transitional devices.

5. Why is editing important?

Chapter 4

Introductions

© Darrin Henry, 2012. Used under license from Shutterstock, Inc.

Key Terms

Introduction method, background information method, general to specific method, anecdote method, contrast method, quote method, question method, surprising statement method

Introduction Purpose

The traditional five-paragraph essay has three parts: the introduction, the body, and the conclusion. This chapter covers the introduction paragraph.

The purpose of the introduction is three-fold:

- Introduce the topic of the essay
- Catch the reader's interest/draw the reader in
- Present the thesis statement

The introduction itself can be broken down into two parts: the introduction method and the thesis statement. An **introduction method** is the way you choose to introduce the topic of the essay and draw the reader in. The **thesis statement** is the main idea of the essay that is expressed in one sentence and is usually the last sentence in the introduction in the traditional five-paragraph essay. Thesis statements are covered in greater detail in Chapter 2.

You should craft your thesis statement before writing your introduction because it is crucial that none of the specific information that will be covered in the thesis appears anywhere else in the introduction. In other words, the first time the specific points that will be written about in the essay appear in the introduction are in the thesis statement.

Furthermore, when writing an introduction or a thesis statement, there are a few things to avoid. First, do not announce. This includes statements like "In this essay, readers will learn . . ." or "This essay will show. . . ." These kinds of statements are unnecessary because they are implied; let your essay speak for itself. Generally, you should not mention the essay or any part of the essay when writing. Therefore, you should also avoid statements like "In this essay" or "In this paragraph."

There are many ways to write an introduction, and below are seven methods you can use when beginning your essay. Notice that in all of them, the thesis statement is the same and is the last sentence in the introduction.

Background Information Method

This method gives historical background information on the topic. The brief background information serves two purposes. One purpose is to draw your reader into the paper by including historical information about a current topic. Another purpose is to show that you are credible and knowledgeable about the topic being discussed.

EXAMPLE

In the mid-twentieth century, television replaced radio as America's main electronic device around which families would gather to spend time together. No longer did families have to just listen to their shows; now they could watch the news and other programs. Originally in black and white and primarily placed in living rooms, TVs now deliver shows in thousands of high definition colors, and today in some homes, there is a television in every room and a television for every person in the house. Families can watch all kinds of programs via local, cable, or satellite channels. Television has many benefits because it is educational, it is entertaining, and it is cheap.

Notice how this particular example includes both historical background information and general information on the topic of television. Then, the thesis statement is presented as the last sentence of the introduction paragraph.

THINK *Write!*

Activity 4.1

1. List two historical details about television that the introduction discusses.

    _____

    _____

2. List two general statements about television according to the introduction.

    _____

    _____

General to Specific Method

The general to specific method is the most common type of introduction. In this introduction method, you begin with a general opening statement and then funnel or narrow the introduction to the thesis statement.

EXAMPLE

In America, just about everyone watches television. Whether it is to escape from reality or to learn something new, people are pressing the on button on the remote control and tuning in. Individuals enjoy viewing a variety of TV programs, including fitness shows, sitcoms, and sporting events. Consequently, TV viewing has become a leisure activity for millions because it offers something for everyone. Television has many benefits because it is educational, it is entertaining, and it is cheap.

THINK *Write!*

Activity 4.2

1. The general opening sentence in the above general to specific introduction lets the reader know that the essay will be about what?

    _____

    _____

2. Then, the thesis statement, which is the last sentence in the introduction, lists the three points that will be developed. What are the three points?

    _____

    _____

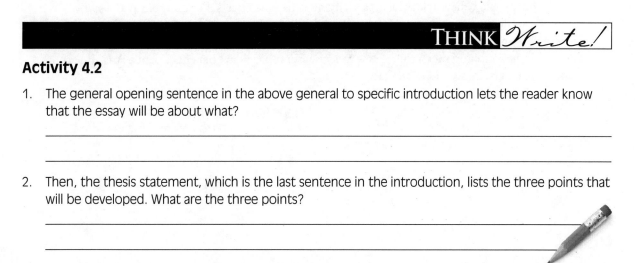

Anecdote Method

An anecdote is a brief story. Therefore, an anecdote method introduces your topic through a brief story that illustrates the topic. These can be written in first person, when you write about yourself and use *I*, *me*, *my*, *we*, or *us*, or third person, when you write about someone else and use *they* or *he/she*. Oftentimes, in academic writing, you will not use first person; however, the writing mode you are working on will determine whether you need to use first person or third person.

EXAMPLE

Everyday Helen plops her three-year-old son, Jeremy, in front of the television set to watch *Sesame Street*. Jeremy sits enraptured while the Muppets dance on the screen, singing and talking in funny voices. Jeremy sings along with them, learning his alphabet and numbers as he does so. He watches the children on the show interact with the Muppets and the adults, and Jeremy learns about manners and behavior. Television has many benefits because it is educational, it is entertaining, and it is cheap.

Above is an example of a third person anecdote. It both introduces the topic of the essay, television, and illustrates the point the writer is trying to make: that television has many benefits. Then, the thesis statement is presented as the last sentence of the introduction paragraph. When using the anecdote method, it is important to note that some reference to the brief story must appear in your conclusion so that you come full circle with the story began in the introduction.

Contrast Method

When the contrast method is used, you summarize the opposite opinion of your own. You do not necessarily agree with the opposite opinion—you are only acknowledging it. After doing so, a key transition word that shows contrast is needed to let the reader know you are now moving to your own opinion. The contrast transition words *however*, *although*, or *but* are generally used for this purpose. This introduction style is particularly good for essays about a topic that has two sides, such as an argument essay.

EXAMPLE

Some people believe television has many negative side effects. For example, people who watch it and do nothing else can become obese. Also, children can become desensitized to violence, and graphic images and foul language can negatively impact young adults. Additionally, television can waste too much time. However, television has many benefits because it is educational, it is entertaining, and it is cheap.

In the example above, the writer begins by acknowledging the opposite opinion. Then, a key contrast transition word is used to signal to the reader that the writer is changing to the writer's own opinion, and the rest of the essay will stay on that side of the topic.

THINK *Write!*

Activity 4.3

1. According to how the above introduction began, what did you think the essay was going to be about at first? _____

   _____

2. What contrast transitional word is used to signal to the reader that the writer is changing to the writer's own opinion? _____

3. What will the rest of the essay be about? _____

   _____

Quote Method

Another way to begin an introduction is to start with a quote. You can use a direct quote, meaning you use quotation marks and attribute where you took the quote from or who said it, or you can use an indirect quote, meaning you summarize the main idea of the quote.

EXAMPLE

"Television! Teacher, mother, secret lover," Homer Simpson once said in loving reverence of his television set on an episode of *The Simpsons*. Truly television has as many uses as he claims. Since the 1950s, America has taken advantage of television's usefulness, and its worth has only expanded. Today television acts as not only "teacher, mother, secret lover" but also as a workout instructor, a relaxation technique, a radio, and more. Television has many benefits because it is educational, it is entertaining, and it is cheap.

Like the other examples, the thesis statement is the last sentence of the introduction. When using the quote method, it is important that you correctly use quotation marks and punctuation. Note that commas and periods go inside of the closing quotation mark unless writing a research paper and citing sources within the sentence. Quotation marks are covered in more detail in Chapters 9 and 18.

Question Method

When using the question method, you ask a question or several questions about the topic in the introduction. A reader will want to read your essay to find out the answer(s) to the question(s). It is crucial that any question you ask in the introduction is answered after reading your essay. Otherwise, the reader will be left wondering and wanting more information. In addition, you should know that questions, besides those used in dialogue, should be limited to the introduction and not appear anywhere else in the essay. Using questions throughout your entire essay makes your essay appear too informal for academic writing.

EXAMPLE

Why do people watch TV for hours? What do they get out of it? Do they watch it to learn new things, to laugh at comedians and sitcoms, or to spend an inexpensive evening at home? If every individual were asked this question, he/she would give a different answer.

However, TV viewers would agree that television has numerous positive attributes. Television has many benefits because it is educational, it is entertaining, and it is cheap.

When using the question methods, you must also avoid the tendency to switching to second person and using the words *you* or *your*. Notice neither of these words is used in this introduction; it is written in third person. The only time the second person pronouns *you* or *your* may be used occurs when you are writing dialogue, meaning you are quoting the exact words someone says, or composing a process or how to paper. However, even when writing a process paper, some instructors still prefer that you do not use second person.

THINK *Write!*

Activity 4.4

1. How many questions are asked in the above introduction? _____

2. Do any of the questions contain the words *you* or *your*? _____

3. When may you use the second person pronouns *you* or *your*? _____
    _____

4. If your instructor allows it, in what kind of paper is it acceptable to use second person (*you* or *your*)? _____

Surprising Statement Method

One of the surest ways to catch your reader's attention is to begin your introduction with an unexpected or surprising fact or idea. This method sparks your reader's curiosity, making him/her want to read the rest of your essay.

EXAMPLE

Over nine million people tuned in to watch some portion of the 2012 three-hour funeral of R&B superstar Whitney Houston, with CNN setting a record with 5.4 million viewers, ten times its normal Saturday viewership, according to the Nielsen ratings. Millions sat transfixed in front of their TVs as a who's who list of entertainers paid tribute to Houston. From actor and *Bodyguard* costar Kevin Costner to singer Alicia Keys, the famous all shared their personal stories about the Grammy-award winning icon. Thanks to the power of TV, all who wanted to were able to be a part of the service and join the fifteen hundred invited guests at the New Hope Baptist Church in Newark, New Jersey, to learn about Houston's roots, to cry, to laugh, and to remember a superstar. Television has many benefits because it is educational, it is entertaining, and it is cheap.

When using the surprising statement method, you must be careful to cite the source if you use specific data rather than common knowledge and to make certain that you do not fabricate, make up any information, in an attempt to catch the reader's attention.

THINK *Write!*

Activity 4.5

Read the introduction below, and then answer the following questions.

Maintaining an excellent credit rating is essential today, not only for receiving good rates on mortgages or car loans, but also for getting a job. Before companies hire someone, they check the potential employee's credit rating. If the rating is good, then the hiring process may continue. However, if the credit rating is poor, many employers will not hire a person regardless of their stellar educational background, their outstanding skills, or their impeccable references. Consequently, individuals must know their credit score, guard against identity theft, and live within their means.

a. The above introduction is an example of which introduction method:

   _____ historical background   _____ general to specific or   _____ surprising statement

   Defend your answer. _____

   _____

   _____

b. According to the thesis statement, what three points will be developed in the essay?

   _____

   _____

THINK *Write!* Review Questions

1. What are the three purposes of the introduction?

2. True/False   Announcements like, "This essay will discuss . . ." or "After reading this essay, you will learn . . ." should be avoided in the introduction and anywhere in the essay.

3. Where is the thesis statement located in the introduction in the traditional five-paragraph essay?

4. Which introduction method tells a brief story?

5. Which method summarizes the opposite opinion before presenting the author's opinion?

5

Chapter

Body Paragraphs

© auremar, 2012. Used under license from Shutterstock, Inc.

Key Terms

Topic sentence, support sentences, concluding sentence

Body Paragraphs

The body paragraphs follow the introduction. In a traditional five-paragraph essay, there are three. The body paragraphs are the meat of the essay, where you develop your point. In the body paragraphs, you explain, elaborate, and support your thesis statement. Each body paragraph is only about one of your three topics and one topic only, and these topics come from the thesis statement. They are the three main points listed in the thesis statement. Developing one point only in each body paragraph helps your ideas stay organized and keeps your reader from becoming confused.

The body paragraphs are made up of three parts: the **topic sentence**, the **support sentences**, and the **concluding sentence**. The topic sentence introduces the topic of the paragraph as well as serves as a link to the thesis by mentioning the topic and controlling idea of the essay. Topic sentences, which state the main idea of the paragraph, generally begin with a transitional device.

Topic Sentences

Below are the three topic sentences for the following thesis statement:

Television has many benefits because it is educational, it is entertaining, and it is cheap.

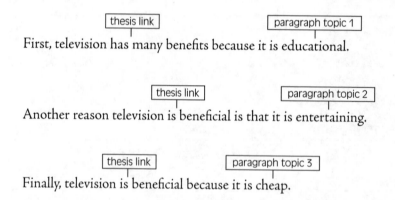

Support Sentences

Following the topic sentence are the support sentences. They give support to the topic sentence by providing details and examples that develop the point the topic sentence is trying to make, which in turn, refers back to the thesis statement. Support sentences are made up of examples, facts, and other details that help you make your point.

First body paragraph: First, television has many benefits because it is educational.

- Children often learn from watching different television shows.
    - They can watch documentaries and cartoons that are geared toward learning.
    - *For example,* the cartoon *Dora the Explorer*, teaches kids to take pride in their heritage, to be adventurous, and to be kind to others.
    - With her friends, Diego and Boots, Dora goes on magical trips to find things or to help others.
- Adults can learn from television, *too.*
    - The Learning Channel, the History Channel, and other channels were specifically created to teach adults about different topics.
    - *For instance,* from these channels, adults can learn to bake, work out, or play a musical instrument.

 🖎 *Furthermore*, adults and children who do not speak English can learn the language from watching American television.

  🖎 They can watch English-speaking shows and learn vocabulary and sentence structure.

  🖎 They can *also* learn pronunciation and dialect.

Concluding Sentences

Notice how the support sentences contain transitional devices to help the reader move smoothly from support to support. After the supporting sentences, the body paragraph wraps up with the concluding sentence. Generally, the concluding sentence restates the topic sentence in some manner and also gives the body paragraph's topic a sense of closure.

CONCLUDING SENTENCES FOR ALL THREE BODY PARAGRAPHS

🖎 There are many educational opportunities with television.

 🖎 Restatement of "First, television has many benefits because it is educational."

🖎 Television can be a great diversion from the daily routine.

 🖎 Restatement of "Another reason television is beneficial is that it is entertaining."

🖎 Television is an inexpensive way to have a good time.

 🖎 Restatement of "Finally, television is beneficial because it is cheap."

FULL BODY PARAGRAPH EXAMPLES

First, television has many benefits because it is educational. [topic sentence] Children often learn from watching different television shows. [support sentence 1] They can watch documentaries and cartoons that teach [specific details for support 1] them to read, to count, and to learn about different cultures and new ideas. For example, the cartoon *Dora the Explorer*, teaches children to take pride in their heritage, to be adventurous, [specific details for support 1] and to be kind to others. With her friends, Diego and Boots, Dora goes on magical trips to [specific details for support 1] find things or to help others. Adults can learn from television, too. [support sentence 2] The Learning Channel, the History Channel, and other channels were specifically created to teach adults about different [specific details for support 2] topics. For instance, from these channels, adults can learn to bake, work out, or play a musical [specific details for support 2] instrument. Furthermore, adults and children who do not speak English can learn the language [support sentence 3] from watching American television. They can watch English speaking shows and learn vocabulary, sentence structure, pronunciation, and dialect. [specific details for support 3] There are many educational opportunities with television. [concluding sentence] [topic sentence] Another reason that television is beneficial is that it is entertaining. There are countless [support sentence 1] dramas broadcast every night on television. [specific details for support 1] For example, HBO's *True Blood* is a popular drama about vampires and other supernatural beings. HBO has other entertaining drama series, as [specific details for support 1] well, such as *Boardwalk Empire*, which takes place during the Prohibition era, and *Game of Thrones*, which is a fantasy series about political intrigue in a feudal society. Viewers can also [support sentence 2] enjoy comedies and sitcoms, like *The Big Bang Theory*, a show about four extremely intelligent [specific details for support 2] "nerds" and their attractive female neighbor. Other comedy examples include *The Office* and [support sentence 3] *Community*. Additionally, reality television keeps the masses entertained. Reality shows cover a [specific details for support 3] wide variety of topics, from following celebrities in their daily lives to competitions. One such [specific details for support 3] competition is *The Voice*, a singing competition on which contestants train with celebrity [specific details for support 3] coaches like Christina Aguilera and Cee Lo Green. Then, they compete against one another to [specific details for support 3] win a recording contract. Shows like this one draw the audience in by making them root for one of the competitors and keep viewers coming back week after week. Television can be a great [concluding sentence] diversion from the daily routine.

[topic sentence] Finally, television is beneficial because it is cheap. Local channels are free of charge and can [support sentence 1] [specific details for support 1] be received with an antenna or a basic receiver box. This includes stations like NBC, ABC, [specific details for support 1] PBS, Fox, and the CW. These basic channels broadcast news shows, one-hour dramas, 30 min- [support sentence 2] ute sitcoms, and educational shows all for free. Cable and satellite, on the other hand, do cost money, but they are cheaper than going to the movies, and there are various packages that can accommodate virtually everyone's price range. Viewers can purchase access to specialized net- [specific details for support 2] [support sentence 3] works, like Nickelodeon, MTV, the Food Network, TNT, ESPN, and Showtime. Lastly, tele- [specific details for support 3] vision can now be accessed online. Viewers can watch their favorite shows on the networks' [specific details for support 3] websites free of charge. Also, sites like Hulu allow viewers to watch some shows for free or to [specific details for support 3] pay a small charge for others. Other services, like Netflix, may be purchased for a nominal fee. [concluding sentence] Television is an inexpensive way to have a good time.

All three body paragraphs are written in this manner. Transitional devices should be used to help move from idea to idea within the paragraphs as well as from body paragraph to body paragraph.

THINK *Write!*

Activity 5.1

Below is a body paragraph excerpt taken from an essay about the importance of going to college. Fill in the missing information.

Another reason obtaining a college degree is important is that it provides more career opportunities. One way it helps is that it _____ . For example, _____ _____ . Also, having a college degree helps with career opportunities because it _____ . For instance, _____ . With a college degree, a person has more advantages than _____ .

THINK *Write!* Review Questions

1. How many body paragraphs does the traditional five-paragraph essay have?

2. What does each body paragraph begin with?

3. What is some of the information that makes up the supporting sentences of body paragraphs?

4. Fill in the blank: Transitional devices should be used to help move from idea to idea within the _____ as well as from body paragraph to body _____ .

5. What does each body paragraph end with?

Chapter 6

Conclusions

Key Terms

Thesis restatement, single sentence method, multisentence method, summary method, suggestion method, prediction method, call-to-action method, revisiting the anecdote in the conclusion

Thesis Restatement Method

The conclusion is the last paragraph in the essay. It is used to summarize your point and bring the essay to a close. No new information should be included in the conclusion.

Usually the conclusion begins with the **thesis restatement**. This means you summarize the main points from the thesis statement using new words. There are a couple of ways to do this.

Single Sentence Method

The original thesis statement should not appear in the conclusion word for word. However, you can re-word the thesis and place it in the conclusion to help summarize the main points of the essay.

EXAMPLE

Original thesis statement: Television has many benefits because it is educational, it is entertaining, and it is cheap.

Thesis restatement: Television is an instructive, enjoyable, and economical device.

Multisentence Method

You can also break up the thesis into several sentences. Generally, the simplest way to do this is to put the topic and the controlling idea into one sentence and then put each of the main points into a sentence of its own.

EXAMPLE

Original thesis statement: Television has many benefits because it is educational, it is entertaining, and it is cheap.

Thesis restatement: Television is very beneficial. There are many ways to educate oneself with television. Additionally, television is a fun way to pass the time. Also, television is inexpensive.

After you have summarized the thesis statement, you need to close the essay in a satisfactory manner. You can do this by using one of the conclusion methods: summary, suggestion, prediction, or call-to-action.

Conclusion Methods

Summary Method

The **summary method** is used to summarize your point one final time.

EXAMPLE

Television audiences can get a lot out of their viewing experiences.

CHAPTER 6: CONCLUSIONS   43

Suggestion Method

The **suggestion method** is used to suggest something to the reader about the topic.

EXAMPLE

Everyone should watch more television.

Prediction Method

The **prediction method** is used to predict something about the topic.

EXAMPLE

In the future, television will continue to teach and amuse Americans.

Call-to-Action Method

The **call-to-action method** calls the readers to get out of their seats and do something about the topic. The call-to-action method is used mainly when writing an argument or persuasive essay.

EXAMPLE

Television audiences should write to television production companies about adding more shows and channels.

TWO FULL CONCLUSION EXAMPLES

SINGLE SENTENCE METHOD

Television is an instructive, enjoyable, and economical device. Americans enjoy watching TV because of what it offers. Television is not only a way to learn new things, but it also allows viewers to have a good time without spending a great deal of money in the comfort of their own home. Television viewers can get a lot out of their viewing experiences.

MULTISENTENCE METHOD

Television is very beneficial. There are many ways to educate oneself with television. Additionally, television is a fun way to pass the time. Also, television is inexpensive. In the future, television will continue to teach and amuse Americans.

Revisiting the Anecdote from the Introduction

Remember in the introduction chapter, you were instructed that if you chose to use the anecdote method, you need to refer back to the anecdote in the conclusion.

ANECDOTE INTRODUCTION EXAMPLE

Everyday Helen plops her three-year-old son, Jeremy, in front of the television set to watch *Sesame Street*. Jeremy sits enraptured while the Muppets dance on the screen, singing and talking in funny voices. Jeremy sings along with them, learning his alphabet and numbers as he does so. He watches the children on the show interact with the Muppets and the adults, and Jeremy learns about manners and behavior. Television has many benefits because it is educational, it is entertaining, and it is cheap.

CONCLUSION EXAMPLE

Three-year-old Jeremy is too young to truly understand all of the benefits that television has to offer. Nonetheless, he, along with other Americans, enjoys watching TV. Television allows individuals to learn and to be entertained in an inexpensive manner. Television audiences can get a lot out of their viewing experiences.

THINK *Write!*

Activity 6.1

Below is an introduction for a process essay on how to maintain a good credit rating.

Maintaining an excellent credit rating is essential today, not only for receiving good rates on mortgages or car loans, but also for getting a job. Before companies hire someone, they check the potential employee's credit rating. If the rating is good, then the hiring process may continue. However, if the credit rating is poor, many employers will not hire a person regardless of their stellar educational background, their outstanding skills, or their impeccable references. Consequently, individuals must know their credit score, guard against identity theft, and live within their means.

On the computer or notebook paper, create a conclusion for the introduction above.

THINK *Write!* Review Questions

1. True/False   The purpose of the conclusion is to summarize the writer's point and bring the essay to a close.

2. True/False   The conclusion is the perfect place to include any information that the writer wanted to include in the essay but could not previously find a spot for it.

3. True/False   The thesis restatement in the conclusion is a word for word restatement of the thesis statement that is in the introduction.

4. True/False   In the multisentence method, the thesis statement is restated in several sentences.

5. True/False   The call-to-action method is a good ending for an argument essay because it encourages the readers to do something.

Below is the complete essay about the benefits of television.

The Positive Attributes of TV

"Television! Teacher, mother, secret lover," Homer Simpson once said in loving reverence of his television set on an episode of *The Simpsons*. Truly television has as many uses as he claims. Since the 1950s, America has taken advantage of television's usefulness, and its worth has only expanded. Today television acts as not only "teacher, mother, secret lover" but also as a workout instructor, a relaxation technique, a radio, and more. Television has many benefits because it is educational, it is entertaining, and it is cheap.

First, television has many benefits because it is educational. Children often learn from watching different television shows. They can watch documentaries and cartoons that teach them to read, to count, and to learn about different cultures and new ideas. For example, the cartoon *Dora the Explorer* teaches children to take pride in their heritage, to be adventurous, and to be kind to others. With her friends, Diego and Boots, Dora goes on magical trips to find things or to help others. Adults can learn from television, too. The Learning Channel, the History Channel, and other channels were specifically created to teach adults about different topics. For instance, from these channels, adults can learn to bake, work out, or play a musical instrument. Furthermore, adults and children who do not speak English can learn the language from watching American television. They can watch English speaking shows and learn vocabulary, sentence structure, pronunciation, and dialect. There are many educational opportunities with television.

Another reason that television is beneficial is that it is entertaining. There are countless dramas broadcast every night on television. For example, HBO's *True Blood* is a popular drama about vampires and other supernatural beings. HBO has other entertaining drama series, as well, such as *Boardwalk Empire*, which takes place during the Prohibition era, and *Game of Thrones*, which is a fantasy series about political intrigue in a feudal society. Viewers can also enjoy comedies and sitcoms, like *The Big Bang Theory*, a show about four extremely intelligent "nerds" and their attractive female neighbor. Other comedy examples include *The Office* and *Community*. Additionally, reality television keeps the masses entertained. Reality shows cover a wide variety of topics, from following celebrities in their daily lives to competitions. One such competition is *The Voice*, a singing competition on which contestants train with celebrity coaches like Christina Aguilera and Cee Lo Green. Then, they compete against one another to win a recording contract. Shows like this one draw the audience in by making them root for one of the competitors and keep viewers coming back week after week. Television can be a great diversion from the daily routine.

Finally, television is beneficial because it is cheap. Local channels are free of charge and can be received with an antenna or a basic receiver box. This includes stations like NBC, ABC, PBS, Fox, and the CW. These basic channels broadcast news shows, one-hour dramas, thirty-minute sitcoms, and educational shows all for free. Cable and satellite, on the other hand, do cost money, but they are cheaper than going to the movies, and there are various packages that can accommodate virtually everyone's price range. Viewers can purchase access to specialized networks, like Nickelodeon, MTV, the Food Network, TNT, ESPN, and Showtime. Lastly, television can now be accessed online. Viewers can watch their favorite shows on the networks' websites free of charge. Also, sites like Hulu allow viewers to watch some shows for free or to pay a small charge for others. Other services, like Netflix, may be purchased for a nominal fee. Television is an inexpensive way to have a good time.

Television is very beneficial. There are many ways to educate oneself with television. Additionally, television is a fun way to pass the time. Also, television is inexpensive. In the future, television will continue to teach and amuse Americans.

PART II

The Writing Modes

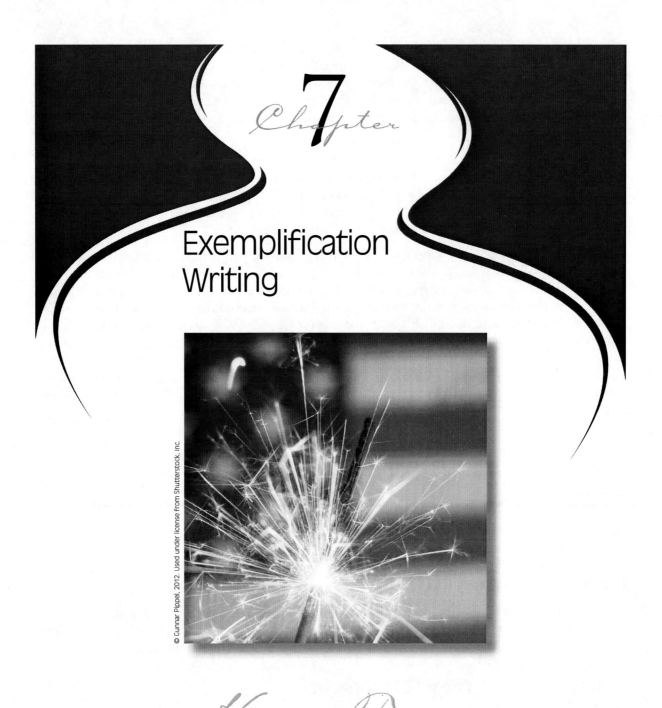

Chapter 7

Exemplification Writing

© Gunnar Pippel, 2012. Used under license from Shutterstock, Inc.

Key Terms

Exemplification writing, first person, third person, extended example, example transitions, addition transitions

When you are asked to clarify or explain a general idea with specific examples, the **exemplification** mode of writing is extremely useful. For example, if you are asked to explain why you should be hired for a summer internship at an accounting firm, you would give examples of skills that would make you the best person for the job. Exemplification essays about aspects of your life, such as experiences, skills, or preferences, are written in **first person**, meaning the pronouns *I*, *me*, *my*, and *mine* are used.

If you are a student in a nutrition class and you are assigned to write a paper on healthy meals that aid in metabolism, you could peruse through a cook book and provide several examples. Depending on whether or not you are allowed to incorporate yourself into the essay will determine whether this exemplification essay is written in first person or third person. **Third person** uses the plural pronouns *they*, *their*, and *them*, and the singular pronouns *he/she*, *his/her*, and *him/her*. Most academic essays are written in third person, so it is imperative that you check with your instructor for clarification.

To begin an exemplification essay, you should start with an introduction paragraph typical of a traditional five-paragraph essay. Therefore, any of the introductory methods discussed in chapter 4: Introductions can be used, such as an anecdote, a quote, or a surprising statement. The body paragraphs also generally follow the format of the five-paragraph essay; each begins with a topic sentence, contains supporting sentences, and ends with a concluding sentence. However, the support for your body paragraphs can be developed by using several related examples, an extended example, or a mixture of both. **An extended example** is a long example that either provides the sole support or the bulk of the support for a body paragraph. The concluding paragraph of the exemplification essay follows the format of the traditional essay: it brings the essay to a close by restating the thesis and then closing out the essay by using one of the conclusion methods.

Exemplification essays use example and addition transitions. Below is a small chart of the example and addition transitions.

Example transitions **help to show examples or illustrate ideas more clearly.**	For example, for instance, including, such as, like
Addition transitions **show additional ideas.**	Also, next, furthermore, another, finally, first, in addition, as well

Exemplification Prewriting

When creating an exemplification essay, you should complete several prewriting strategies, such as free writing, listing, clustering, asking questions, outlining, and building a pyramid, to help you generate ideas. If you get stuck while writing, you can return to the prewriting strategies to generate additional ideas.

Exemplification Thesis Statement

The thesis statement states the main idea of the essay and the three topics that are developed with specific examples in the rest of the essay.

Exemplification Body Paragraphs

Each body paragraph begins with a topic sentence that states one of the three topics listed in the thesis statement. Then, numerous supporting sentences follow. These supporting sentences provide specific examples that develop the topic. The examples can be one long example that is developed throughout the body paragraph or several short examples. A concluding sentence ends each body paragraph.

Conclusion Paragraph

The conclusion paragraph lets the reader know that the exemplification essay is coming to an end. Various techniques can be used to end the essay.

Exemplification Outline

The format of an exemplification essay is the same as a standard five-paragraph essay. Below is a basic outline.

I.   Introduction
   a.   Introduction method
   b.   Thesis statement containing the three topics that will be developed

II. Body 1
   a.   Topic sentence for main point 1
   b.   Example or examples
   c.   Supporting details
   d.   A concluding sentence

III. Body 2
   a.   Topic sentence for main point 2
   b.   Example or examples
   c.   Supporting details
   d.   A concluding sentence

IV. Body 3
   a.   Topic sentence for main point 3
   b.   Example or examples
   c.   Supporting details
   d.   A concluding sentence

V.   Conclusion
   a.   Thesis restatement
   b.   Conclusion method

EXEMPLIFICATION ESSAY EXAMPLE 1

Anticipated Holidays

Just about everyone enjoys celebrating holidays. Holidays allow individuals to get time off from work, to have gatherings, to welcome in a new year, or to honor or remember loved ones who have died. Every year I look forward to my favorite holidays. They allow me to honor one of my heroes and to spend time with my family. Three meaningful holidays I enjoy celebrating are Martin L. King, Jr. Day, Mother's Day, and Father's Day.

One of the holidays I enjoy celebrating is Martin L. King, Jr. Day. On this day, one of the greatest Americans of all times is honored. My family and I celebrate this day by attending at least one of the numerous events. For example, we participate in the city-wide march held in

Dr. King's honor, attend a Monday morning church service that pays tribute to Dr. King's life and legacy, or go to the Meyerson Symphony Center where an annual musical tribute to Dr. King is held. Last year Grammy award winning gospel singer Yolanda Adams was the featured performer. She was backed by a two-hundred-member mass choir comprised of choir members of area churches. Many people view this day as simply a day off, but I see it as an opportunity to show my respect for a great leader who sacrificed his life for others.

Another of the holidays I anticipate is Mother's Day. On this day, I am treated like a queen. My husband, Brian, and our son, Malik, have to wait on me all day long. Whenever I need something, I just ask one of them, and they have to do it on this day. For example, if I am feeling cold, one of them must get me a blanket and spread it out over me. If I cannot reach the remote control, one of them must turn the channel for me and then hand me the remote control. After church, they make breakfast, do the dishes, and make plans for dinner. They either take me out to eat or cook. They usually choose to cook because the lines are so long at restaurants on Mother's Day. My favorite meal for dinner that they make consists of some of my favorite foods, such as salmon, baked potatoes, broccoli, French bread, and salad. For dessert, they serve me apple turnovers and Blue Bell vanilla ice cream. I love this day because I do not have to do any work—everything is done for me.

The third holiday I look forward to is Father's Day. Because our father lives in Ft. Worth and my sister and her family live in Murphy, and my family and I live in Mesquite, we drive to Ft. Worth and celebrate there. We either eat at Papadeauxs Seafood Restaurant or have brunch at a Ft. Worth downtown hotel. On this day, I honor my father, my husband, and my brother-in-law Jeff with a card and gifts. For instance, this past Father's Day I gave my dad a hat and a golf shirt to go with it, I gave my husband a gift card to JC Penney, and I gave my brother-in-law a framed picture of him and my nephew Aaron that was taken at Christmas. I enjoy spending time with the special fathers in my life.

Holidays are special days that are spread out throughout the year. They allow me to do a variety of things from honoring heroes to spending time with those I cherish. Every year I always look forward to celebrating MLK Day, Mother's Day, and Father's Day. These holidays allow me to pay tribute to a leader, to be treated like royalty, and to show how much I love some of the dads in my life.

THINK Write!

Activity 7.1

Answer the following questions about "Anticipated Holidays."

1. Is the essay written in _____ first person or _____ third person?
2. Which introductory method is used?
   a. Historical background
   b. General to specific
   c. Anecdote
   d. Contrast
3. Underline the thesis statement.
4. Underline the three topic sentences and circle the transitional words.

5. List three specific examples of how the author celebrates MLK Day.

_____

_____

6. List some of the specific ways the author is treated like a queen on Mother's Day.

_____

_____

7. List some of the specific examples regarding how the author celebrates Father's Day.

_____

_____

8. Place an asterisk by the concluding sentences of each of the three body paragraphs.
9. In the conclusion, does the author restate the thesis in one sentence or three sentences? _____
10. Which method of conclusion is used to close the conclusion?
    a. Summary
    b. Suggestion
    c. Prediction
    d. Call-to-action

EXEMPLIFICATION ESSAY EXAMPLE 2

College Student of the Year

"And the award goes to . . ." is the phrase that precedes someone's happiest moment and several other people's disappointing moment. However, before individuals can anticipate having their name called, they must be nominated. Each year peers, colleagues, supervisors, or fans seek out individuals worthy of being honored. At college campuses, administrators, professors, staff members, and fellow students nominate an outstanding student. Although the criteria for being nominated Student of the Year differ from college to college, the end result is the same: recognizing students whose achievements exceed those of their peers. Jasmine Morales is the perfect candidate for the Student of the Year award because she is intelligent, helpful, and involved.

One reason Jasmine should win the award is that she is very smart. For example, during her two years at the University of Michigan, Jasmine has maintained a 4.0 GPA. This is an outstanding feat in itself; however, it is even more worthy of recognition because Jasmine is a double major: nursing and international business. Last semester Jasmine was not certain that she would receive all A's because she was struggling in Chemistry 1402. Instead of bemoaning her predicament, she took action. She met weekly with her chemistry professor, Dr. Nguyen, during her office hours and spent two hours in the tutoring center every day. Focused and determined to not only learn the material but master it, Jasmine went from a C+ average to an A in the course. Jasmine's pristine academic record is definitely an achievement worthy of recognition.

Her willingness to help her fellow students at the university is another reason Jasmine deserves to win the Student of the Year award. For instance, when her English professor asked for someone to volunteer to be the scribe for a student with limited mobility with his hands, Jasmine immediately agreed to assist the student. Not only does she take notes for the student, but she also meets him on Saturdays at the computer center and assists him in typing up his essays. Another example of her helpfulness is her willingness to give one of her History 1302 classmates a ride to the campus two days a week. After she overheard her fellow classmate explaining to their professor that she was late on Tuesdays and Thursdays because she had to wait for her son's school bus to pick him up before she could catch her own bus to the college, Jasmine offered to give her classmate a ride to campus. Jasmine's willingness to assist her peers is remarkable.

The third reason that Jasmine is the perfect choice for the award is that she is involved in numerous campus organizations. For example, she is the student government treasurer, co-captain of the girls' intramural soccer club, and historian of the international business organization. As vice president of the nursing club, Jasmine spearheaded a health fair that provided free pregnancy and HIV/AIDS testing for students. One of her favorite extracurricular activities, however, is serving as the program chair of the salsa club. In this capacity, Jasmine is responsible for not only finding opportunities for the club to dance but also for securing volunteer opportunities for the members on and off campus. For instance, last week Jasmine arranged for the club to dance in a Cinco de Mayo celebration at the college's satellite campus and to assist in the letter writing campaign, "Thank the Troops," for their service to the country, sponsored by the college's Veterans' club. An off campus volunteer opportunity for the salsa club that Jasmine is spearheading will begin this fall. Two Friday afternoons a month the club will read to students at Cesar Chavez Elementary.

Jasmine Morales deserves to win the Student of the Year award. Her academic work is impeccable. In addition, her altruism she displays in her willingness to help her fellow classmates is commendable. Also, her commitment to being involved in campus organizations at such a high level is exceptional. Not only should Jasmine win this award, but in the future, she will probably win the Outstanding Alumna award, too.

THINK *Write!*

Activity 7.2

Answer the following questions about "College Student of the Year."

1. Which introductory method is used?
   a. Anecdote
   b. Contrast
   c. Quote
   d. Question

2. Underline the thesis statement.

3. Which topic sentence has the transitional device toward the end of the sentence instead of the beginning? _____

4. How is the first body paragraph developed? _____ several examples, _____ several examples and an extended example, _____ only an extended example

5. How is the second body paragraph developed? _____ several examples, _____ several examples and an extended example, _____ only an extended example

6. How is the third body paragraph developed? _____ several examples, _____ several examples and an extended example, _____ only an extended example

7. Which body paragraph is missing a concluding sentence? _____ 1st, _____ 2nd, _____ 3rd

8. Write a concluding sentence for the missing body paragraph:

   _____

   _____

9. On notebook paper, define the following words: *altruism, alumna, bemoaning, impeccable, pristine*

10. Which method of conclusion is used?
    a. Summary
    b. Suggestion
    c. Prediction
    d. Call-to-action

THINK *Write!*

Activity 7.3

Fill in the missing information for the exemplification outline about dangerous jobs.

Thesis Statement

Three of the most dangerous jobs that people risk their lives daily for others are fire fighters, police officers, and soldiers.

Topic Sentence Body Paragraph 1

I. One example of a dangerous job is that of fire fighters.
   a. Burning buildings
   b. _____
   c. _____

Topic Sentence Body Paragraph 2

II. _____
   a. Get shot at
   b. _____
   c. _____

Topic Sentence Body Paragraph 3

III. Soldiers also have extremely dangerous jobs.
   a. Get shot at
   b. _____
   c. _____

Exemplification Essay Topics

1. What are some examples of why people get divorced?

2. Why should you or someone else win Employee of the Month, Spouse of the Year, or Parent of the Year?

3.   What is the worst or best job you ever had?

4.   What are some annoying habits people have?

5.   What are three things you are afraid of?

6.   What are three fun, nonviolent video games?

7.   What are some bizarre superstitions?

THINK *Write*/ Review Questions

1.   What does exemplification writing use to provide specific details in the body paragraphs?

2.   Define extended example.

3.   What is the difference between first person and third person?

4.   List four example transitions.

5.   List two addition transitions.

8 Chapter

Descriptive Writing

Key Terms

Descriptive writing, dominant impression, sensory details, figurative language, simile, metaphor, personification, onomatopoeia, space order

The purpose of **descriptive writing** is simple: to create a vivid image in the reader's mind using only words. When you use descriptive writing, you will pile on so much description that the reader will have no trouble picturing the topic in his/her mind. Descriptive writing should be dripping with details, to the point where it almost seems like too much, but it never is: the more descriptive detail in descriptive writing, the better.

Example Thesis Statements without Points Listed

With any essay, you must first express a clear thesis statement before beginning to write the essay.

> My garden is lovely.

> New York City is dirty.

It is crucial that you establish a dominant impression in the thesis statement because it is the controlling idea of a descriptive essay. The **dominant impression** controls the rest of the essay based on the impression you want the reader to perceive. Therefore, in the case of the garden, you will only write about lovely things, like flowers, green grass, and butterflies. You will not mention the weeds trying to choke the rose bush. That would be outside the dominant impression and would not be included. Along the same lines, the New York City essay would only be about the dirty parts of the city; you would not mention how pretty Central Park is.

Once you have established the dominant impression, you can now think of three main points about the topic and controlling idea to discuss in the body paragraphs. The descriptive essay follows the traditional five-paragraph format: introduction, three body paragraphs, and a conclusion. Therefore, you need three main points to be the topics of the three body paragraphs. These can either be listed as a part of the thesis statement or can be left off depending on your professor's preferences or instructions. The examples above have left off the three main points.

Example Thesis Statements with Points Listed

Below are examples of thesis statements with the points listed.

> My garden is lovely because of the flowers, the vegetables, and the trees.

> New York City is dirty because of the garbage, the cars, and the buildings.

As with other five-paragraph essays, the thesis statement will almost always be placed as the last sentence in the introduction.

In the body paragraphs, strong, clear topic sentences are needed to tell the reader what the paragraph is about. Then, you must provide enough descriptive detail to make the reader visualize the topic in his/her mind. This can be done using **sensory details** and **figurative language**. Sensory details are vivid descriptions appealing to the reader's five senses. Many times, you tend to only rely on sight to describe something, but sight alone is not going to allow the reader to truly picture the topic in his/her mind. You also need to describe sound, touch, taste, and smell.

THINK *Write!*

Activity 8.1

Sight

Describe the following picture using only sight details. How run down is this house? What do you see?

_____

_____

_____

_____

_____

Sound

Describe the following picture using only sound details. Think about volume and time between sounds.

_____

_____

_____

_____

_____

Smell

Describe the following picture using only smell details. Imagine the numerous foul odors. How would you describe them? Can you use a comparison?

_____

_____

_____

_____

_____

_____

_____

Touch

Describe the following picture using only touch/feel details. Think about texture. How does the skin feel? What about the tusk? What about the feet?

© Four Oaks, 2012. Used under license from Shutterstock, Inc.

_____

_____

_____

_____

_____

_____

_____

Taste

Describe the following picture using only taste details. Think about the words used to describe food, like rich or sweet.

© Aleksandr Stennikov, 2012. Used under license from Shutterstock, Inc.

_____

_____

_____

_____

Figurative Language

To strengthen the sensory details, you can use figurative language. There are many figurative language devices you can use to do this, including **similes, metaphors, personification,** and **onomatopoeia.** A **simile** is a comparison using "like" or "as" to help describe something.

EXAMPLES

The day was as hot as the sun.

The pool felt like a cool drink of water.

These two examples appeal to the reader's sense of touch. They strengthen the sensory details with comparisons. The reader knows the day was extremely hot, but the pool felt cool and refreshing. **Metaphors** are similar to similes, but they do not use "like" or "as" when comparing. Instead, they say one thing *is* another thing as a point of comparison. Although similes are easy to use, metaphors usually present a stronger image for the reader.

EXAMPLES

The river was a snake.

The house was an old man.

With these two examples, the reader immediately gets images in his/her mind. The river is curvy and winding; the reader knows this because it has been called a snake. Because the house has been compared to an old man, the reader knows it is probably stooped or leaning with peeling paint and faded colors. Next, **personification** is giving inanimate objects or ideas human characteristics. Doing this can usually give the reader a powerful image in his/her mind because the reader can relate to the human characteristic being portrayed.

EXAMPLES

The leaves danced in the wind.

The smell climbed out of the old well.

Because of the personification, the reader understands that the leaves in the example above are moving gracefully and rhythmically. They are not being tossed around by the wind or shaken furiously. The smell, on the other hand, is climbing, which gives the sense that it is coming slowly out of the well, up to the reader's nose, like it is creeping. It is almost a little eerie, like it is after someone, because things do not normally climb out of wells. Last, **onomatopoeia** is used when words sound like the sounds they are describing. They can be just a single word, creating a sound, or used as a verb to create the sound.

EXAMPLES

The thunder and lightning *crashed.*

The fire *crackled* merrily.

Bang!

Boom!

Onomatopoeia is good to help you create sound details for the reader. A good way to remember onomatopoeia is to think of them as the *Batman* words. In the old *Batman* television show with Adam West, every time Batman had a fight with a villain onomatopoeia would appear on the screen: Pow! Bam! Bang! Onomatopoeia is also used often in comic books and graphic novels.

THINK

Activity 8.2

Use the suggested figurative device to describe the items below. Write the onomatopoeia as a complete sentence.

1. The ocean (metaphor)

   _____

   _____

2. The Corvette Stingray (simile)

_____

_____

3. The football stadium (onomatopoeia)

_____

_____

4. The library (metaphor)

_____

_____

5. The tree branches (personification)

_____

_____

6. The old barn door (onomatopoeia)

_____

_____

7. The computer (onomatopoeia)

_____

_____

8. The rock (simile)

_____

_____

9. The algae (personification)

_____

_____

10. A baby (simile)

_____

_____

When composing a descriptive essay, you generally uses **space order**. Space order is describing how things relate to one another in a space. For example, if you were describing your college, you might write about the library being above the computer lab and how the writing classrooms are at the front of the school. Space order requires the space transitions. Below is a small chart of the space transitions. Use the space transitions to help you move from one idea to another within a body paragraph. It is also acceptable to use other transitional devices, like addition or example transitions.

Space transitions **show direction or location.**	In front, in front of, behind, next to, beside, above, around, between, by, down, in, near, on, over, toward, under, to the right, to the left

Descriptive Prewriting

In addition to using any prewriting strategies—free writing, listing, clustering, asking questions, outlining, and building a pyramid—you should draw on your senses to help generate ideas. If possible, you can refer to a picture of what you are describing, go to the place, or meditate on the experience before attempting to prewrite.

Descriptive Thesis Statement

The thesis statement consists of two parts: the topic and the dominant impression. The three points that you will discuss may or may not be listed.

Descriptive Body Paragraphs

Each body paragraph begins with a topic sentence that states one of the three topics that supports the dominant impression. Then, numerous supporting sentences that are loaded with sensory details follow. These supporting sentences help convey the dominate impression. Remember for the descriptive essay the more sensory details the better. Figurative language like similes, metaphors, and personification also helps in conveying a clear picture for the reader. A concluding sentence ends each body paragraph.

Conclusion Paragraph

The conclusion paragraph restates the dominant impression and lets the reader know that the descriptive essay is coming to an end. You can use various techniques to end the essay.

Descriptive Outline

The format of a descriptive essay is the same as a standard five-paragraph essay. Below is a basic outline.

I.   Introduction
    a.   Introduction method
    b.   Thesis statement containing a dominant impression

II. Body Paragraph 1
    a.   Topic sentence for main point 1
    b.   Sensory details
    c.   Figurative language
    d.   Concluding sentence

III. Body Paragraph 2
    a.   Topic sentence for main point 2
    b.   Sensory details
    c.   Figurative language
    d.   Concluding sentence

IV. Body Paragraph 3
    a.   Topic sentence for main point 3
    b.   Sensory details

    c.   Figurative language

    d.   Concluding sentence

V. Conclusion

    a.   Thesis statement restated, including dominant impression

    b.   Conclusion method

DESCRIPTIVE ESSAY EXAMPLE 1

Crimson and Burnt Orange

In early October every year, the Red River Rivalry is held at the original Cotton Bowl in Fair Park in Dallas, Texas. This football game between the University of Oklahoma and the University of Texas is highly anticipated every year by Sooner and Longhorn fans alike. It is played in Dallas because it is considered "neutral ground" for the two teams, each traveling approximately two hundred miles to reach Fair Park. Tickets can cost hundreds of dollars, and people scalp them for even more. The Red River Rivalry is fun because of the fans, the stadium, and the fair.

First, the fans make the Red River Rivalry an entertaining experience. They come dressed in their teams' colors: Sooners in crimson and cream and Longhorns in burnt orange and white. The Sooners are a red river flowing into the stadium, and the Longhorns look like a wildfire. Everyone is loud and raucous, shouting school chants and taunting and jeering at the opposing team. Inside, the fans are all crowded in like sardines, packed shoulder to shoulder, but that is part of the fun. They eat nachos smothered in bright orange cheese and drink hoppy smelling beer and bottled water that is cool on the tongue. When the Sooners score, the OU fans roar with triumph, and the Ruf/Neks, OU's men's spirit group, fire their shotguns with a loud crack. If the Longhorns score, the fans scream and shout with joy, and the Texas Cowboys, one of UT's men's spirit groups and service organizations, let UT's canon, Smokey, boom. Some of the biggest fans of the teams are the two university marching bands. The horns flash in the sun, and the cymbals are shiny gold coins. The drummers pound the snares and basses, creating a pulsing beat. The music of both bands parades around the stadium merrily, weaving in and out of the crowd like a dancer. The fans sway and move like a sea of grass in the wind. The exuberant fans make the Red River Rivalry a blast.

Next, the stadium and its field are integral parts of the enjoyment of the Red River Rivalry. The Cotton Bowl is big and old, and it is amazing to know that Sooner and Longhorn fans have gathered there for over a century of football games. The seating is split 50/50, so half the stadium is crimson and half is burnt orange. The seats are shiny and silver and filled with a diverse group of people. Some seats are practically in the clouds whereas others are right on the sideline. Inside, delicious smells from the concession stands waft through the corridors, and lines for the water fountain and bathroom stretch for miles, but it is worth it in the end. Next, the field below is painted as green as an emerald with bright white lines to mark the boundaries of the game. The south end zone is a deep red, and the north end zone is a rusty orange. The replay screen up in the south end zone is a giant, looming over the OU side of the field and casting a shadow that helps fans find relief from the sun. Down on the field, the players fight to win the game. Footballs arc like rainbows across the green grass, and the running backs are cheetahs rushing across the field to catch them. The defense plows through the offense, trying to sack the quarterback. The fans roar with approval, and the sound echoes off the stadium's high walls. The Cotton Bowl is a fun place for the Red River Rivalry.

Finally, no matter who wins the game, fans flow out of the stadium to enjoy the State Fair of Texas. It seems everyone is always starving after the game, and a "victory corny dog" is a must. The breading is crisp and greasy and delicious, and a streak of tangy mustard tops it all off. There are other things to try as well: turkey legs, brisket, Indian tacos, and gyros. The smell of grease hangs in the air like a fog, making the stomach growl. For a sweet treat, some fans get a sticky caramel apple or a deep fried dessert, like a fried Oreo or Twinkie. Others go for funnel cakes covered in powdered sugar like fairy dust. After filling themselves up, fans can head indoors to check out shows and get out of the heat. A myriad of cars are housed in one building, looking like an auto salesman's show room. Another building houses a petting zoo. The llamas are soft like cotton, and the piglets oink and squeal. Afterward, it is time for rides. The Ferris wheel, called the Texas Star, presides over the state fair like a queen, wheeling lazily in the dusky fall sunlight. There are small roller coasters and rockets, tilting ships and gentle carousels. The rides bob up and down, crash and whiz and whirl, playing music like wind-up toys, old gramophones, and huge boom boxes. Brakes hiss as the rides stop, and seat belts click as people unbuckle them to get off. As the sun dips beneath the horizon, the fair lights blink on. They are a rainbow of colors, twinkling like stars in the night sky. The fair is one of the best parts of the Red River Rivalry.

The Red River Rivalry is a must see for all Sooners and Longhorns. It is an event like no other and has to be experienced firsthand. The fans, the stadium, and the fair make it a fabulous time. In the future, Oklahoma and Texas teams and fans alike will continue to gather at the Cotton Bowl every October to battle it out.

THINK *Write!*

Activity 8.3

Answer the following questions about "Crimson and Burnt Orange."

1. Which introduction method is used?

   _____

2. Underline the thesis statement. Does it include the main points listed?   Yes/No

3. Underline any figurative language you find. Between the lines above the words, write what type of figurative language device is used.

4. List any sensory details you find below for each sense:

   a. Sight: _____

   _____

   _____

   _____

   _____

   _____

   _____

   _____

   _____

b. Sound: _____

_____

_____

_____

_____

_____

_____

_____

_____

_____

c. Smell: _____

_____

_____

_____

_____

_____

_____

_____

_____

d. Touch: _____

_____

_____

_____

_____

_____

_____

_____

_____

    e.   Taste: _____

_____

_____

_____

_____

_____

_____

_____

_____

_____

5.   Underline the thesis restatement. Is it the single sentence method or the multisentence method?

_____

6.   Which conclusion method is used?

_____

THINK *Write!*

Activity 8.4

Fill in the missing information for the pyramid below for a descriptive essay titled "My Abuela's Kitchen."
Try to come up with two additional supporting details.

My Abuela's Kitchen is filled with love.

Homemade food	her listening ear	the mementos from her grandchildren
Tamales	relationship blues	handmade art work

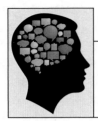

THINK *Write*/TIP

Descriptive writing can be used in more than just the descriptive essay. Its elements can cross over into other writing modes, like the narrative. As you continue to grow as a writer, you can use elements of descriptive writing for different types of assignments. Additionally, descriptive writing can even be used across disciplines.

DESCRIPTIVE ESSAY EXAMPLE 2— STUDENT ESSAY BY DOROTHY BENNETT

Big Bend

I fell in love with the Big Bend area of Texas when I visited there in 1991. I was there to inspect forty acres I had purchased so that I could have access to a rare multicolored king snake known to live in that region. My land is located only eleven miles north of the Big Bend National Park. The rugged terrain is hard to navigate, but the trip is always worthwhile. The Big Bend area is uniquely beautiful because of its mesmerizing skies, its secluded peacefulness, and its arid grandeur.

The skies of the Big Bend area are mesmerizingly beautiful. I would have to say that God used His entire palette of colors here. At sunrise, the eastern sky breaks with beams of golden yellow. Slowly, the sun pushes back the dark night, and the midnight blue becomes lighter and brighter. After spending a day under a crystal blue sky, the sunsets are an event to behold. The deep bruise purples and the burnt oranges mix with splashes of bright pink fuchsia to cover the entire scope of the western horizon. Then, as moonlight replaces sunlight, the stars come out by the millions. They fill the sky so completely it looks like lace hanging down in gossamer ribbons toward the sleeping earth. The air is so clean one can watch satellites as they pass in their orbits around the globe. It is truly hard to tear one's eyes away from Big Bend's big skies.

The secluded peacefulness is another appealing feature of the Big Bend area. The quiet is thick and tangible. It wraps everything in a plush blanket. There is no sound; only the wind dares to speak. Loneliness is not the feeling that is conveyed though. Instead, there is a communion with nature, the earth, and the sky. There is the impression of being an important part of a grand plan. Peacefulness seeps into the pores like sunshine through a screen. Being over one hundred miles from the nearest town should cause fear, but the tranquility of the land brings serenity. Breathe deep, be still, and enjoy the isolation.

Finally, the arid grandeur of the Big Bend area is breathtaking. There are pale purple mountains along the horizon in every direction. The vegetation is a muted sage color, as if all the plants are covered in dust. The heat bakes out of the sparsely covered ground and makes everything shimmer with mirages. The weather is extreme. The temperatures soar to the 100s by day and plummet to the 50s at night. When it does rain, there is usually a flash flood, but even then the ground does not become muddy. The rain goes through the sand like a sieve, barely leaving enough moisture to keep the snakes, lizards, and cacti alive. The thirsty scenery drinks the water out of the air. It is a beauty that, if not respected, could bring a tragic end to its beholder.

The beauty of the Big Bend area is unique. It has skies that hold one spellbound. The quiet is palpable and wise. The dry splendor of the terrain takes my breath away. I will be returning to this land of enchantment as often as I can.

THINK *Write!*

Activity 8.5

Answer the following questions about "Big Bend."

1. Which introduction method does the writer use?

    _____

2. Underline the thesis statement. Does it include the main points listed?   Yes/No

3. Underline any figurative language you find. Between the lines above the words, write what type of figurative language device is used.

4. List any sensory details you find below for each sense:

    a. Sight: _____

        _____

        _____

        _____

        _____

        _____

        _____

        _____

        _____

    b. Sound: _____

        _____

        _____

        _____

        _____

        _____

        _____

        _____

    c. Smell: _____

        _____

        _____

        _____

        _____

        _____

        _____

        _____

d. Touch: _____

_____

_____

_____

_____

_____

_____

_____

_____

e. Taste: _____

_____

_____

_____

_____

_____

_____

_____

_____

5. Underline the thesis restatement. Is it the single sentence method or the multisentence method?

_____

6. Which conclusion method is used?

_____

Descriptive Essay Topics

1. A place: a night club or a restaurant

2. A person you love

3. A place to watch a sporting event, concert, or theatrical play

4. A room in your home

5. A place of worship

6. A restroom, kitchen, or locker room

7. Your ideal boyfriend/girlfriend, spouse, or significant other

8. A photograph

THINK *Write!* **Review Questions**

1. Define the purpose of descriptive writing.

2. Define dominant impression. Why is it important?

3. Define sensory details.

5. Define simile, metaphor, personification, and onomatopoeia.

5. Define space order and give two examples of space transitions.

9
Chapter

Narrative Writing

Once Upon a Time...

Key Terms

Narrative writing, time order, 5WH, foreshadowing, showing and not telling, scene, pacing, conflict, dialogue, tense shifts

Narrative writing is a part of everyday life. Books are narratives and so are movies. Television series are narratives, as well. This is because narratives are stories, and narrative writing is storytelling. A narrative essay, then, is a story *that has a point*. This means you, the writer, learned something from the experience you are writing about and you want to share it with your reader. It does not have to be profound or deeply meaningful, but you must have a reason for telling the story. For example, if you chose to tell the story of how you climbed a mountain despite a fear of heights, the point would be that you overcame the fear and accomplished something. Narratives without points are extremely boring and have a tendency to ramble on without actually going anywhere; the point keeps the narrative focused. In other essays, the point is included in the thesis statement. However, the narrative's format is not that of the traditional five-paragraph essay. Instead, it is more free form, and you will not reveal the point until the end of your narrative.

To begin a narrative, you should start with an introduction paragraph similar to that of a traditional five-paragraph essay. However, narrative essays do not use the traditional thesis statement. Instead, after you have introduced the story, you place a foreshadowing sentence as the last sentence of the introduction. **Foreshadowing** is a literary device used to hint to the reader that something is about to happen. It will draw the reader in and keep him/her reading. Foreshadowing in a narrative essay hints at what you will learn from the experience.

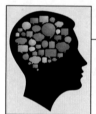 THINK *Write!*/TIP

> Much of the formal, academic writing you do in college avoids the use of first person (*I, me, my, mine*). Narratives, however, can be written in first or third person. Many times instructors ask students to write personal narratives, which means that it is acceptable for you to use first person, and oftentimes you are expected to do so in narrative writing.

Example of Background Information and Foreshadowing

The Camping Nightmare

I had always enjoyed camping. My family and I camped all throughout my childhood at different sites around the state. It was always so fun to spend time enjoying the outdoors, cooking over the fire, fishing, and swimming. When I got to college, I thought camping over spring break with friends was an excellent idea. **Unfortunately, this turned out to be one of the worst experiences of my life.**

In this example, the writer gives some background information on herself. Thus, the reader knows the writer considers herself an experienced camper. Therefore, the foreshadowing statement is intriguing, pulling the reader in. How could it have been such a bad experience if the writer is an avid camper? The reader must now continue reading to find out.

After the introduction, you tell your story from beginning to end. This is called **time ordering**. Time order requires time transitions to help move from idea to idea inside the story. Below is a chart of time transitional devices.

Time (chronological) transitions **show the order in which events occur(ed).**	First, next, before, after, then, as, during, immediately, later, meanwhile, now, often, previously, suddenly, when, while, second, third, last, finally

As you write the narrative, you may take as many paragraphs as needed to tell the story. Therefore, there will not just be three body paragraphs like in a traditional five-paragraph essay. There can be five, six, seven, or even eight. The narrative essay is as long as it needs to be to get your story told. Additionally, your paragraphs do not have to be a certain number of sentences. Paragraphs that include dialogue, for example, may be only one or two sentences while paragraphs that give descriptive detail might be five, six, or more.

Narrative Elements

5WH

You need to include a few elements when writing a narrative essay. The first element is the **5WH**, which are the important elements of the story. 5WH stands for who, what, where, when, why, and how. Who is in the story? What is happening? Where and when? Why and how? If one of these key elements is missing, your reader has lost important information.

Conflict

Narratives also need to have **conflict**. Conflict is a problem or issue occurring in the story. There are three different kinds of conflict: human vs. human, human vs. nature, and human vs. self. Without conflict, stories become extremely boring. When you see a movie where nothing happens, you are often mad afterward and feel like you just wasted your time. That is how a reader feels after a narrative without any conflict. Without conflict, nothing is going on.

The Scene

At the beginning of a narrative, you introduce the topic with a foreshadowing sentence and then set the scene with any background information necessary for the reader to understand what is happening. All of this is written in summary, meaning there is not much descriptive detail. Then, it is time for the **scene**. A scene is the place where the action of your story occurs. It is the middle of the story, and it is also where the conflict of the narrative happens. Scenes should include lots of descriptive detail. You can also include dialogue. Scenes are not meant to cover days at a time from your life; they are usually fifteen minutes or less. Even though it is such a short time in your life, much of the narrative is spent describing and explaining what happened during this moment. This is called **pacing** because the beginning and end of the story are summarized at a quick pace, whereas the scene is taken at a slow pace, including as much detail as you possibly can. The majority of your paragraphs in a narrative are written about the scene.

Showing versus Telling

During the scene, it is important for you to "show and not tell." **Showing and not telling** is giving a reader descriptive detail to help him/her imagine the scene taking place. Telling is boring and too quick of a pace for a scene. Showing is dripping with detail and allows the reader to imagine what is going on; it is somewhat similar to the use of descriptive detail and figurative language from descriptive writing. Look at the example below to see the difference between telling and showing.

Telling: Bob was angry, so he left.

Showing: Bob's eyes narrowed, and a deep frown creased his face. For a moment, he stared at me, his expression as cold as ice, but then he stormed out of the room, slamming the door behind him with a loud bang.

The difference is immediately apparent. When "telling" occurs, the reader knows what happened, but it is hard for the reader to imagine it or visualize it clearly in his/her mind. "Showing" does a much better job of this and also requires more writing and more sentences.

THINK *Write!*

Activity 9.1

With a group, partner, or on your own, turn these "tell" sentences into "show" descriptive passages.

Lisa was sad.

_____

_____

_____

_____

Miguel's broken arm hurt.

_____

_____

_____

_____

Dialogue

Something else you can include in a narrative scene is dialogue. You use dialogue when one person or several people in the story speak. Dialogue is not always necessary, but it is also sometimes essential to the story. Dialogue requires specific punctuation and format when it is used.

1. **When two or more people talk back and forth to one another, start a new paragraph each time you switch from one person to another.**

   "The day that you agreed to be my wife was the happiest day of my life," Roberto said. "I am so happy that you chose to marry me. With you, I have everything that I will ever need."

   "Roberto, I am grateful for your love," Josephina replied.

   "What would I do without you?" Roberto asked.

   Josephina answered, "You will never need to find out because our love will last forever. If we are parted by death, we will see each other again someday."

2. **If only one person speaks, make the quotation part of the paragraph; do not indent it.**

   Roberto shows his love for his wife through the things he says and does. For example, the first words and the last words that Roberto says to his wife every day are these, "Josephina, I love you. I am so grateful that you agreed to be my wife." Although he says these words every day, Josephina never gets tired of hearing them because they reaffirm daily that her husband loves her. Besides declaring his love for her, Roberto shows his love by putting it into action. For example, he writes his wife love letters, runs her bath water, and brings home flowers and candy, not just on Valentine's Day, but at least once a week. Roberto definitely loves his wife.

3. **Periods and commas go inside of the closing quotation mark.**

   Roberto said, "I love only you."

   "I love only you," Roberto said.

4. **If one person speaks for several sentences, only use one set of quotation marks. In other words, put the opening set of quotation marks at the beginning of the first sentence. Then, put the closing quotation marks at the end of the last sentence. DO NOT PUT OPENING AND CLOSING QUOTATION MARKS at the beginning and ending of each sentence.**

   In a disappointed tone that I will remember forever, Julie said, "I cannot believe that you cheated with my boyfriend. I thought that you were my friend. I will never trust you again."

5. **Make certain that if your dialogue/quote ends with a question mark, the A in asked is lowercased.**

   "Where are you going?" asked John.

   John asked, "Where are you going?"

THINK *Write!*

Activity 9.2

Correct the five dialogue errors below.

RaShawn asked "Dad, can I borrow the car?"

His father replied, "Yes, you can, but you must fill it up with gas, wash it, vacuum out the inside, and drop your little sister off at her friend's house".

"By the time I do all that, the party will be over, RaShawn whined.

RaShawn's dad smiled and said, I'd be glad to drop you off and pick you up."

"Ok, RaShawn responded in a defeated tone.

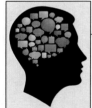

THINK *Write!* TIP

Usually you write narrative essays in past tense because they are often about something that happened in your life in the past. Therefore, it is important to check verb tense as you write the narrative essay. It is very easy to shift into present tense when writing a narrative because when you tell a story aloud, you oftentimes use present tense. However, when writing a narrative, you need to make sure to stay in past tense if the event you are writing about happened in the past. After you finish the narrative, it is important to go back and edit for **tense shifts**, which are times when you accidentally change from one verb tense to another while you are writing. As a writer, you must always maintain a consistent tense no matter what mode you are writing.

Narrative Essay Prewriting

Because of the organization of the narrative essay, you may find that the prewriting strategy free writing helps you generate ideas easier. As you free write, you can pour out your story onto the page and then go back and decide which points you want to develop more and which ones you want to leave out.

Narrative Thesis Statement

The thesis statement for the narrative essay consists of the foreshadowing sentence. This sentence, located at the end of the introduction, hints that something is about to happen. It should intrigue your reader to want to read the rest of the essay to find out what happens.

Narrative Body Paragraphs

Unlike the standard five-paragraph essay, the narrative contains more than three body paragraphs. The narrative contains as many body paragraphs as you need to tell the story, to answer the 5WH, and to develop the conflict—meaning your narrative could have five or more body paragraphs. In addition, the body paragraphs do not begin with traditional topic sentences or end with concluding sentences. The rules for body paragraphs are suspended for the narrative because stories do not fit into the standard body paragraph format. You can make new body paragraphs when the action slightly changes, when some time elapses, when the paragraph is getting too long, or when dialogue is used.

Conclusion Paragraph

In the conclusion paragraph, you reveal the point of your story if you have not done so already. If you have revealed the point, then you reiterate the point or the lesson learned.

Narrative Outline

The format of a narrative essay differs from the standard five-paragraph essay. Below is a basic outline.

I.   Introduction
    a. Introduction method
    b. Foreshadowing sentence

II.   Body Paragraph 1
    a. Development of 5WH, the scene, and the conflict
    b. Showing not telling

III.   Body Paragraph 2
    a. Development of 5WH, the scene, and the conflict
    b. Showing not telling

IV.   Body Paragraph 3
    a. Development of 5WH, the scene, and the conflict
    b. Showing not telling

V.   Body Paragraph 4
    a. Development of 5WH, the scene, and the conflict
    b. Showing not telling

VI.   Body Paragraph 5
   a.   Development of 5WH, the scene, and the conflict
   b.   Showing not telling

VII. Body Paragraph 6
   a.   Development of 5WH, the scene, and the conflict
   b.   Showing not telling

VIII. The number of body paragraphs continues until the story is told.

IX.   Conclusion
   a.   The point of the story is revealed
   b.   The narrative comes to the end

NARRATIVE ESSAY EXAMPLE 1

The Soccer Trauma

At sixteen and after over ten years of playing soccer, I figured I was a pretty smart player. After all, I was a starting forward on both my competitive team and the varsity team at my high school. I had pulled hat tricks, I could get past just about any sweeper, and I had the endurance and the strength to play the entire game without a substitute. However, I was soon to discover that I had at least one more lesson to learn.

On the Sunday before Thanksgiving of 1999, my team was playing our biggest rival in the competitive league, Velocity, at the soccer fields in Plano. We had never beaten them, and I had decided it was because Velocity had this huge sweeper, a blond girl who was about a mile tall, and none of our forwards could get past her. She was very intimidating, looming over us and casting a shadow as long as the field, but I had decided that today would be the day I would get past her. I would not be afraid of her anymore, and we would win.

The game began. I waited for my opportunity to challenge the sweeper, and finally it came. One of our defenders booted the ball over the half line where I was waiting, and I took off after it at top speed.

There she was, running after the ball at top speed too. She seemed even bigger than ever and moved a lot faster than I would have imagined she could. Her face was a mask of concentration, her blue eyes focused hard on the ball that was bouncing between us.

I narrowed my eyes. I was not going to be afraid of her. My team was counting on me to get that ball. I picked up my speed and pushed myself harder. As I did so I could hear the coach and my parents and other spectators cheering me on, and this just made me want it more.

We reached the ball at the exact same time. We both kicked it, our feet hitting the ball at the exact same moment. I kicked with the side of my foot, as though I were passing the ball, because I wanted to pull the ball slightly to the left. She kicked with her shoelaces to boot the ball as far away from her goal as she could. The forces at which we kicked, equally powerful, trapped the ball between us for a moment.

When this happened, our feet also stopped abruptly, but because of how I had placed my foot sideways, my knee kept going, ripping violently forward. A moment later the ball popped out from between us and flew toward their goal in the waning fall sunlight. I had won the ball, but I could not go after it because the force of my encounter with the giant sweeper had sent me somersaulting onto the ground.

As soon as I stopped, sprawled on Velocity's goal line, I knew something was wrong with my knee. At first, it lost feeling. The numbness was strange and disconcerting, but then pain flared up suddenly, causing tears to form in my eyes. It felt as though something inside my knee had come unhinged. When I tried to walk, my knee would barely bend. I had to be carried to the car to be taken to the minor emergency room.

It turned out I had torn cartilage in my knee, and I eventually needed corrective surgery to bend it again. I was told that had I kicked the ball with my shoelaces, it would not have happened. Kicking the ball with the side of my foot had caused my knee to jerk sideways as well, and when my foot stopped and my knee kept going, my meniscus tore. I continued to play soccer and I continued to challenge other players, but never again did I use the side of my foot when facing off with a defender; it was shoelaces from then on.

THINK *Write!*

Activity 9.3

Answer the following questions about "The Soccer Trauma."

1. Underline the foreshadowing sentence.
2. How many body paragraphs are there? _____
3. Highlight any "showing and not telling."
4. What paragraph does the pacing slow down?

   _____

5. What paragraph ends the scene?

   _____

6. What is the conflict in this story?

   _____

7. What is the 5WH?
   Who: _____
   What: _____
   Where: _____
   When: _____
   Why: _____
   How: _____

8. Dialogue is not used in this narrative. Do you think adding dialogue would enhance or detract from the story?

   _____

9. What is the point of this narrative? What did the writer learn? Where is the point placed in the narrative?

   _____

NARRATIVE ESSAY EXAMPLE 2

In the narrative below, an inanimate object tells a story about itself. In other words, personification—giving inanimate objects human characteristics—has been expanded upon as the author becomes a crystal paperweight and writes a first-person narrative about a traumatic event in its, the object's, life. Elements of descriptive writing have also been used.

The Disappointed Crystal Paperweight

When I was fashioned out of a block of the finest crystal, I knew that I was destined for greatness. Due to my beauty and the flower etched in me, I had no doubt that I would reside on a high-powered female executive's immaculately clean glass top desk, where the sunlight would reflect off of me and humans would admire my workmanship and sheer loveliness. Unfortunately, life had other plans for me.

I will never forget the day Monsieur Dumont, my creator, lovingly spoke these words: "Crystal flowers numbered one through ten thousand, it is time for you to leave this place and to go out into the world. You are to be the protectors of great pieces of paper that will impact many people's lives."

After this powerful proclamation, I was gently placed in my own black velvet box, wrapped in white tissue paper, and shipped to my new home. I, along with twenty-five hundred others, was transported to Neiman Marcus in downtown Atlanta. Although on the outside I looked just like the others, I knew that I deserved special treatment because on the inside I knew I was superior.

Since it was Christmas time, elegant and expensive items, such as myself, were leaping off of shelves and out of the store's revolving doors. We were to be given as gifts to people's loved ones, employees, coworkers, adopted families, and themselves.

When I was purchased by a sophisticated woman wearing a Donna Karan pinstriped suit, I thought that I would shatter into a zillion pieces because I was so excited. She clearly had exquisite taste because she selected me out of all of the paperweights in the entire store. I was confident that I would be the envy of all my siblings because I was definitely purchased by someone who—clearly by her suit and the BMW trunk that she placed me in—had a great deal of class like myself.

My self-importance quickly faded when she took me to work with her the next day. Instead of having her car valet parked in front of a high-rise office tower, she parked her own car in a packed college parking lot and scooped up her other gifts that she had purchased for her co-workers and friends. I was given to an intelligent and witty but very messy colleague of hers who greatly appreciated me and then immediately buried me under a stack of students' essays.

Instead of resting in plain view on a sunlit top executive's desk, I am hidden in an overworked professor's windowless office. Every day I dream of what might have been. My sad tale supports the adage: "Pride goeth before a fall."

THINK *Write!*

Activity 9.4

Answer the following questions about "The Disappointed Crystal Paperweight."

1. Underline the foreshadowing sentence.
2. How many body paragraphs are there? _____
3. What purpose does the dialogue play in the narrative? _____
    _____
4. Where does the conflict occur? _____
5. What is the point of the story? Where is it located? _____
    _____
6. On notebook paper, define the following words: *adage, etched, exquisite, immaculately, proclamation.*

NARRATIVE ESSAY EXAMPLE 3— STUDENT ESSAY BY DOROTHY BENNETT

The First Time I Slept with a Rattlesnake

In the late eighties and early nineties, I was married to Arnold, and he was a snake collector. He had enjoyed the hobby since he was a young boy growing up in the deserts of California. I found the animals intriguing and beautiful, so I had no qualms about keeping snakes, lizards, and spiders of all kinds in our home.

My husband and I were a part of a group that would take trips to west Texas looking for the rare gray-banded king snake. On one trip, we were driving the roads between Del Rio and Marathon looking for snakes that would come to the blacktop to get warm after the sun had set. We had collected quite a few unusual snakes, including a magnificent six-foot-long western diamondback rattlesnake, so we headed back to our campsite located just outside of Comstock. We brought everything we caught into the tent with us at night so that the snakes would not get overheated in the truck. We kept them in pillowcases that we tied into a knot at the top, or, rather, at least we tried to keep them there.

After we had been asleep for a few hours, I started having the most vivid dream of my life. I dreamed that I was lying next to Arnold in our tent, and the view was exactly what I would see if I just opened my eyes: the angle of the tent wall; the light coming through the window from the campground outside; the color of my sleeping bag. Everything was precisely as it would be in real life, and hovering just a few inches from my face was the head of the six foot diamondback we had caught earlier that evening. It was coiled in that famous "S" shape they make right before they strike. I was not frightened; it was quite beautiful with very distinct markings in many shades of brown, a gray that was almost purple, and bright white.

Soon, I started getting a funny feeling that maybe this was not a dream after all. I sat straight up and grabbed the flashlight. I looked around the tent and over at the bags of snakes and saw nothing out of place and certainly not a six foot rattlesnake. I turned off the flashlight, laid it down, and went back to sleep.

The next thing I knew, it was dawn, and Arnold was telling me, in a very strange tone, to be still. Apparently that was no dream because I had laid the flashlight down right on top of the six foot snake. Arnold started trying to move it away from me, just in case I could not stay still, but he had no need to be worried; I was a stone.

Of course, the snake did not like being prodded and poked that way, so it started rattling. It was so loud it hurt my ears. Everyone in the campground heard it, and they all came running. Arnold said, "Okay, you can move now," and any part of my body that made contact with the ground *pushed*. I swear, even my breast launched me backward. I scrambled out of the way and out of the tent. I stood outside the door flap and watched as Arnold re-bagged the snake. My adrenaline was pumping so hard that I had not even noticed that I was naked until one of our friends put a blanket around me.

I learned two valuable lessons on that trip. From then on, I made all of our bags myself. I would sew them into extra long pillowcase shapes, then turn them inside out, and double stitch around the edge. I never used anyone else's bags again. No matter how beautiful they were, some of the things we collected were deadly. We needed to remember that, regardless of how much fun we were having.

I also learned that I should trust my intuition. I thought I was dreaming, but it was my mind showing me what was really happening. I could have died that night, but God had other plans.

THINK *Write!*

Activity 9.5

Answer the following questions about "The First Time I Slept with a Rattlesnake."

1. Underline the foreshadowing sentence. (Hint: This essay has a two-paragraph introduction.)
2. How many body paragraphs are there? _____
3. Highlight any "showing and not telling."
4. What is the conflict in this story?

   _____

5. What is the 5WH?

   Who: _____

   What: _____

   Where: _____

   When: _____

   Why: _____

   How: _____

6. A small amount of dialogue is used in this narrative. Would more dialogue have been useful here or detracted from the story?

   _____

7. What is the point of this narrative? What did the writer learn? Where is the point placed in the narrative?

   _____

Narrative Essay Topics

1. Write about a time you were frightened, experienced prejudice, or were angry. What did you take away from this encounter?

2. Write about a time that was embarrassing when it happened but is humorous now when you think about it.

3. Discuss a time when you were disappointed by someone close to you. How will you avoid this same situation or something similar from happening again?

4. Discuss a time you regret. What did you learn from the situation?

5. Write about a significant moment in your life: your graduation from high school, your wedding day, the birth of a child, or the funeral of someone close to you.

6. Tell the story of an inanimate object.

THINK *Write*/ Review Questions

1. What is the purpose of narrative writing?

2. Define scene.

3. Define pacing.

4. Define 5WH.

5. Define conflict.

6. Define tense shifts.

10
Chapter

Process Writing

© alterfalter, 2012. Used under license from Shutterstock, Inc.

Key Terms

Process writing, fixed order, loose order, implied "you," second person, tone

Process writing explains how something works or how something is done. Every day you use processes as you navigate through your life. Several processes are often done unconsciously and in no formal order. There are some processes, however, that you must do in a particular order following specific directives, such as changing a car tire or performing a tonsillectomy.

When writing a process essay on how something is done, you should choose a topic that you know a great deal about because you are considered "the expert"—meaning your essay must contain all of the information needed for someone to follow your advice. You must include in your list of steps tips to help the reader know if he/she is doing the procedure correctly, why it is important to follow this advice in the first place, what happens if this advice is not followed, what precautions should be taken, and what problems could occur. Besides providing steps that are clear and easy to follow, you have the added responsibility of making the writing interesting as well.

Fixed Order and Loose Order ✓

Before beginning the process essay on how something is done, you must decide how your list of steps will be followed. If the list of steps must be done in a specific order, then the process requires a **fixed order**. On the other hand, if the steps can be arranged in various ways, then you can use **loose order**.

THINK *Write!*

Activity 10.1

Decide if the following process essays would require a fixed or a loose order of steps. In the blank, write F for fixed and L for loose.

1. _____ changing a baby's diaper

2. _____ driving defensively

3. _____ planning a surprise party

4. _____ baking a cake

5. _____ setting up a tent

Second or Third Person

In most essays, you have to choose between writing in first or third person. First person means you use the pronouns *I*, *me*, *my*, and *mine* whereas in third person you use the plural pronouns *they*, *them*, and *their* and the singular pronouns *he/she*, *him/her*, and *his/her*. However, when writing the process essay, your choice is between second or third. Unlike any other mode, process essays sometimes use the **second person** pronoun *you*. This means that you, the writer, are talking directly to the reader. If the word *you* appears in the essay, that means it is directly stated. In contrast, if the word *you* does not appear but it is understood to have been used, then the *you* is **implied**. Commands that begin with verbs that are complete sentences have the implied *you* as the subject.

EXAMPLES

Sit down.

Arrange the screws from longest to shortest.

Be quiet.

Turn on the computer and wait for it to boot up.

Join a club on campus.

THINK *Write!*

Activity 10.2

Identify the following as a fragment or a command. If it is a fragment, put an F in the blank. If it is a command with the implied "you," put a C. Note that some commands begin with an adverb instructing how to complete the command.

1. _____ Standing by the door.

2. _____ Quickly slide the credit card.

3. _____ Glue the shape to the poster board.

4. _____ Silently counting to ten before speaking.

5. _____ Consider the alternative.

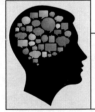

THINK *Write!* TIP

Be aware that sometimes the implied *you* sneaks into your essays when you are not writing a process essay. Therefore, you must double check any of your sentences that begin with verbs that have you talking directly to the reader or instructing the reader to do something.

Tone ✓

Although most process essays are written in a serious tone, they can be humorous or zany. For example, topics such as how to sabotage a date or how to become your professor's favorite student forever could be written in a humorous or zany, over the top tone. The **tone**, which is the style or manner in which a work is written, must remain consistent throughout. This means that if your process essay begins in a serious tone, you should avoid humor so that your reader knows these are genuine steps that can be followed to accomplish something. However, if your process essay begins in a humorous tone, it should be humorous throughout; otherwise, the reader will be unsure if the essay is meant to be funny and taken lightly and not followed.

Checklist for Process Writing

Before beginning a process essay, you must answer the following questions.

1. What do I know about that I can explain to others in a clear and interesting manner?

2. What will the tone of my essay be: serious or humorous?

3. Will I use you, the implied "you," a mixture of both, or third person?

4. What are the most important steps in my process?

5. Will the steps in my process essay be fixed or loose?

6. What order will I arrange my steps?

7. What tips can I provide so that the readers know they are completing the steps correctly?

8. What are some pitfalls or precautions readers need to know about?

Process essays primarily use time and addition transitions.

Time (chronological) transitions **show the order in which events occur(ed).**	First, next, before, after, then, as, during, immediately, later, meanwhile, now, often, previously, suddenly, when, while, second, third, last, finally
Addition transitions **show additional ideas.**	Also, next, furthermore, another, finally, first, in addition, as well

Process Essay Prewriting

Because steps are needed for the process essay, the prewriting strategy listing would be a good place for you to start generating ideas. You could create a vertical list of the steps needed to do something. Then, you could go back and group like ideas together using numbers as instructed when creating a super list and scratching out irrelevant ideas. Refer back to Chapter 1: Prewriting. Grouping the ideas will help you create the major steps.

Process Thesis Statement

The thesis statement lets the reader know what process you will be writing about. If only three steps are needed, then you can list the steps in your thesis statement so that you include the plan of development. If, however, more than three steps are needed to complete the process, then you should use a general thesis statement as the last sentence of the introduction. A general thesis statement lets your reader know what process you are writing about, but it does not include the plan of development. For example, if you were writing a process essay about how to plan a vacation and you had five steps, your thesis statement could be the following: If you want to plan a stress-free vacation, you should follow these five steps. Then, your reader would have to wait until each of the five body paragraphs to find out the specific tips.

Process Body Paragraphs

The body paragraphs of the process essay explain your steps. Each body paragraph begins with a transitional device and a clear topic sentence that states the step you will discuss in that paragraph. Be sure to include tips on how to perform each step and precautions to take. Each body paragraph ends with a conclud-ing sentence.

Conclusion Paragraph

In the conclusion paragraph, you restate the thesis and reassure the reader that if the steps are followed as instructed, he/she will be successful.

Process Outline ✓

The format of a process outline is the same as the standard five-paragraph essay as long as only three steps are included. If more than three steps are included, then additional body paragraphs will be needed. Below is a basic outline.

I.   Introduction
   a.   Introduction method
   b.   Thesis statement containing the three steps that will be discussed

II. Body Paragraph 1
   a.   Topic sentence for the first step
   b.   Explanation of the step/supporting details
   c.   Tips/precautions
   d.   Concluding sentence

III. Body Paragraph 2
   a.   Topic sentence for the second step
   b.   Explanation of the step/supporting details
   c.   Tips/precautions
   d.   Concluding sentence

IV. Body Paragraph 3
   a.   Topic sentence for the third step
   b.   Explanation of the step/supporting details
   c.   Tips/precautions
   d.   Concluding sentence

V.   Conclusion
   a.   Thesis restatement
   b.   Conclusion method/summarize the steps or instructions for the process

PROCESS ESSAY EXAMPLE ✓

The Weight Battle

Do you battle with your weight? Have you tried more than two diets in the past year? Are you aware that many people in the United States are overweight? In fact, America is one of the fattest countries in the world, and Texas is in the top percentile of fat states. Even more alarm-ing, Dallas' population of obese people has skyrocketed, and now the city is considered one of the fattest in the state. Therefore, it is time to start losing weight. Three simple steps will have you on your way to a lighter you. You can begin to lose weight by making better food choices, counting calories, and exercising.

The first step in weight loss is making better choices with the food you eat. Before you even begin doing anything else, take an inventory of the food you eat every day. The best way to do this is to keep a food diary for a few days. Record every morsel of food that goes into your mouth, including what you drink and "taste" off of your spouse's, child's, or friend's plate. This can be very enlightening, especially if you suddenly realize you "graze" all day long and eat fast food every evening. Obviously, that has got to stop. Then, check what you have in your refrigerator and pantry. Are they full of junk food and snacks? Those have got to go, too. Once you have done this, head out to the grocery store and pick out some healthier items like fruits, vegetables, and sports drinks. You can also get healthy snacks, including certain chips and chocolates. This way you still get what you want to eat; it is just the healthy version instead. Making healthy food choices will be tough at the beginning, but it will become easier over time.

The second step to your weight loss success is calorie counting. Even if you are eating healthier, you can still consume too many calories. To figure out how many calories a day you should be eating, you can go online and use a calorie maintenance calculator. This will tell you how much you have to eat on a daily basis to maintain your current weight. After you know this number, you can subtract a certain amount to help yourself lose weight. Generally, however, no one should eat less than twelve hundred calories a day. Eating too few calories will cause the body to go into starvation protection mode, causing your body to try to preserve or store what you intake to preserve your strength and proper functioning of your vital organs. Although you are counting calories, you do not become a slave to doing so because that may cause you to become obsessive and upset if you exceed your set calorie intake amount. If you do go over the limit one day, simply avoid eating dessert the next day to get back on track. Absolutely do not tell other people how many calories that slice of chocolate cake or that milkshake is unless they ask you. You do not want to be slim and trim and friendless. Counting calories is important, but remember to keep it in perspective.

Finally, you must exercise to lose weight. If you have not exercised in a very long time, it is best to start slow. Walk around the block two or three times a week. Eventually, you can add more days. Once you have gotten used to that, up your workouts and start jogging. You can also join sports teams and play soccer, softball, baseball, or football. Joining a gym is a good idea too, so you have access to both cardio equipment, like treadmills and elliptical machines, and also weight training equipment. If you join a gym, you can even get a personal trainer to help you with your weight loss goals. If joining a gym is not in your budget, work out with a family member or friend. Working out with someone helps to keep you motivated to exercise. Once exercising becomes part of your routine it will become a habit that you enjoy doing, not only to lose weight but also to keep your body in motion.

Losing weight can be accomplished if you follow the right steps. First of all, make better food choices. Secondly, count your calories. Lastly, you must exercise. Following these steps will soon have people asking, "What have you been doing? You look marvelous!" Go ahead and give these steps a try. You will not regret it.

THINK *Write!*

Activity 10.3

Answer the following questions about "The Weight Battle."

1. Is "The Weight Battle" written in second or third person? _____
2. Which introduction method is used? _____
3. What is the thesis statement of the essay? Write it in the space provided below.

_____

_____

4. Underline the three topic sentences and circle the transitional devices in each.
5. Is this process essay in a fixed order or a loose order? _____
6. List one precaution that each body paragraph contains.
   Body paragraph #1: _____

   Body paragraph #2: _____

   Body paragraph #3: _____

7. Place an asterisk by the three commands or the sentences that use the implied "you" in the conclusion.

THINK *Write!*

Activity 10.4

The thesis statement from "The Weight Battle" has been revised so that it can be used in a third person process. Fill in the missing information.

Thesis: If people want to lose weight, they should make better food choices, count calories, and exercise.

Topic Sentence #1: The first step people should follow is to make better food choices.
Topic Sentence #2: _____

_____

Topic Sentence #3: _____

_____

Process Essay Topics

1. How to kick a bad habit—smoking, cussing, biting one's nails
2. How to break up with someone (make it serious or humorous)

3. How to be named Employee of the Month

4. How to succeed in college

5. How to use Twitter or another social media

6. How to get along with your neighbor/how not to get along with your neighbor

7. How to sabotage a date

THINK *Write*/ Review Questions

1. What are the two persons that process essays can be written in?

2. Explain fixed and loose order.

3. What is the implied "you"?

4. True/False   Process essays must always be serious.

5. List some of the transitions used in a process essay.

11
Chapter

Argument Writing

© iQoncept, 2012. Used under license from Shutterstock, Inc.

Key Terms

Argument writing, tactful, pro and con list, opposing viewpoints, a stance, parallel structure, call-to-action

Oftentimes when you hear the word argument, you automatically think about negative experiences you have had in the past. The argument could have stemmed from disagreements that got out of hand, causing you to feel that an argument was warranted in order for you to get your point across. Although you may have had reasons for feeling so strongly about the topic of discussion, most times arguments are not well thought out, planned, or organized. When writing in an academic setting, it is imperative that planning and organization exist from beginning to end. When writing an argument, it is important to know that there is a tactful way to get your opinion across about controversial topics without offending the reader. **Tactful** refers to thinking about what you say or write before you say it or write it, as well as thinking about how others will perceive what you say or write. The information in this chapter encourages you to use helpful strategies that can be used across all domains of your life.

Argument writing is a way for you to express your opinion about a topic and try to convince others to take you side. In other words, arguments are meant to persuade your readers to agree with you and question their own thinking about their opinions.

Pro and Con Lists

Sometimes when you are asked to write an argument essay, you may feel overwhelmed and not know where to begin or how to generate ideas. One quick way to get the writing process started is to create a **pro and con list**. This informal listing technique can be done alone, in pairs, or in groups. The goal is to generate reasons for (pro) something and reasons against (con) something so that you can generate possible ideas to write about. In addition to serving as a way to generate ideas, a pro and con list also helps you come up with arguments that the opposition would make if you are required to or choose to address the **opposing viewpoints** in your argument essay. The opposing viewpoints are the arguments that are the opposite of what you are developing in your essay that some of your readers will have.

To create a pro and con list, draw a line down the center of the page. Then, label one side "Pro" and the other side "Con." Next, start listing ideas on either side as they come to mind.

Below is a pro and con list for deciding whether or not parents should spank their children. As you create your pro and con list, do not worry about parallelism, right or wrong answers, or repetitive answers; the goal is to generate ideas.

Pro (Reasons for spanking children)	Con (Reasons against spanking children)
Parents were spanked as kids	Parents hated being spanked as kids
Teaches discipline	Causes kids to fear their parents
Children learn to respect authority	Causes emotional problems
Biblically based (spare the rod . . .)	Spankings versus beatings
A valid form of discipline	Some parents spank too hard
A good consequence for misbehavior	A form of abuse
A form of tough love	Teaches kids to hit others
It works!	Causes mental harm
Fear cuts down on misbehavior	

After creating a pro and con list, you should examine it and see if you can find three reasons (points) to write about. Unless specifically told to write about one side or the other, you are free to choose to write about either the pro or the con side. However, under no circumstances are you able to straddle the fence, meaning be on both sides or a quarter on one side and three-fourths on the other—you must clearly be on one side or the other. Depending on the issue, sometimes it is actually easier to argue the opposing side of what you believe because some points may jump out from the opposing viewpoints that cause ideas to start forming in your mind. Other times it is easier to argue the opposing side if you are too emotional about an issue and are unable to be objective or tactful. Ultimately, you should base your decision on which side you feel you can argue more effectively.

THINK *Write!*

Activity 11.1

On notebook paper, create a pro and con list for one of the following argument prompts.

- ✍ Should using a cell phone while driving be illegal?
- ✍ Are child beauty pageants exploitive?
- ✍ Should the alcohol age be lowered/raised?
- ✍ Should elderly family members be placed in nursing homes?

Taking a Stance

When writing an argument, you must take a **stance** or a position about a topic and not waiver. Even if in actuality you are in the middle of an issue, when you write the argument essay, you must choose a side and stay on it. Otherwise, the argument will not be effective. The words "should" and "should not" are often used in an argument essay's thesis statement because they clearly communicate your stance.

In Chapter 2: Drafting, you learned the function of a thesis statement and how important thesis statements are regarding the coherence of the essay. Argument writing is no different. The main function of a thesis statement for an argument essay is to state your opinion about a topic and provide the reader with reasons for why you believe the way you do.

Parallel Structure

When creating the thesis statement, you must double check that your thesis statement possesses parallel structure. **Parallel structure** refers to similarity in words and phrases. This means that all items in a list are "balanced" or "match" in regard to parts of speech. In other words, all items in a list contain –ing words, to + a verb, verbs, nouns, adjectives, adjectives + nouns, phrases, or complete sentences.

Below is an example of a parallel thesis statement for an argument essay that was created after generating a pro and con list.

> **Parents should not spank their children because it causes emotional, mental, and physical harm.**

The thesis statement states the topic (**spanking**), offers the writer's stance (**parents should not spank their children**) and three reasons (**emotional, mental, and physical harm**).

THINK *Write!*

Activity 11.2

Using ideas generated from the pro and con list, complete the thesis statement below that is in favor of spanking children. Make certain the three points are parallel.

Thesis: Parents should spank their children _____

_____

_____

_____

_____

In argument essays, no first person pronouns like *I, my, me, mine, we, our,* or *us* are used in the thesis statement or anywhere in the essay. Therefore, you absolutely cannot use any of the following phrases: "I think . . . ," "In my opinion, . . . ," or "I feel. . . ." Using any of these phrases weakens your argument because the entire essay expresses your opinions. Instead, you simply state the topic, your opinion about the topic, and three reasons.

THINK *Write!*

Activity 11.3

Using ideas generated from the pro and con list, complete the thesis statement below that is against spanking children.

Thesis: Parents should not spank their children _____

_____

_____

_____

_____

After the thesis has been constructed correctly, the reader should be clear about your stance and which side you will argue in the essay.

The introduction of an argument essay should do the following: introduce the topic, give the reader any necessary background information about the topic, and provide the reader with a thesis statement that specifically shows your stance about the topic and the three reasons.

For argument essays, you can use any of the introductory methods from Chapter 4: Introductions. Below is an example of an anecdote introduction for the argument essay "Spare the Children."

Spare the Children

Several children were playing by the lake one Sunday afternoon. Everyone was having fun. One child fell into the lake and got his Sunday clothes drenched. He began crying profusely as he saw his father walking toward him. The boy's father took his belt off and began to spank his son repeatedly. Afterward, the boy looked around sobbing only to see his friends watching in disbelief. Weeks after the incident occurred, the boy began to perform poorly at school and was sent to the principal's office for fighting. When asked why he was behaving so badly, he had nothing to say. Eventually the little boy told the school counselor that he felt depressed. He admitted that his parents spanked him often and that he wanted to run away. The little boy's parents were unaware that the spankings were having a negative effect on their son. Parents should not spank their children because it causes emotional, mental, and physical harm.

Furthermore, you may incorporate the following strategies to create an introduction that acknowledges the opposing viewpoint.

1. Be polite: Insulting readers will lessen your chances of captivating an attentive audience.

2. Provide examples of how the opposing viewpoint and yours are the same: This may put the readers at ease and consequently make them convert to your viewpoint.

3. Show where your and the opposing opinions are different: This will strengthen your argument by revealing to you weaknesses in the opposing argument.

4. Recognize the opposing argument: This will show that you are a rational person.

Below is an example of an introduction for the argument essay "Spare the Children" that addresses the above tips.

Spare the Children

For several centuries, parents have thought that corporal punishment was a way to discipline children. During biblical times, people believed that it was a mandate from God to not spare disobedient children from harsh physical punishment. Proponents of spanking state that spanking children teaches them how to be respectful toward authority. Furthermore, some parents believe that because they were spanked as children they should instill the same values into their own children. Granted, no one wants disobedient children, and some children who are spanked do change their negative behavior and refrain from repeating certain offenses; however, today there are healthier and more effective forms of discipline besides spanking. Most importantly there are negative consequences that result from spanking children. Parents should not spank their children because it causes emotional, mental, and physical harm.

After you have an effective introduction that contains a thesis statement that states your stance and three reasons, you are ready to compose the three body paragraphs. Each of the three body paragraphs will develop one of the points from the thesis. Specific support is needed so that you express your argument in a well-thought out manner. The supporting details should include evidence, facts, observations, and examples. No sweeping generalizations or insulting language should be used because that will cause your reader to stop reading and dismiss your argument as irrational. The conclusion of an argument essay brings the essay to a close by using a restatement of the thesis. The **call-to-action** method is often used to end the argument essay. This conclusion method calls your readers to get out of their seats and do something about the topic. Refer to Chapter 6: Conclusions.

Argument essays use time, addition, cause and effect, contrast, and example transitions. Below is a chart of the transitions.

Time (chronological) transitions **show the order in which events occur(ed).**	First, next, before, after, then, as, during, immediately, later, meanwhile, now, often, previously, suddenly, when, while, second, third, last, finally
Addition transitions **show additional ideas.**	Also, next, furthermore, another, finally, first, in addition, as well
Cause and effect transitions **show the effect of something.**	Therefore, as a result, as a consequence of, because, since, consequently, so, thus, ultimately, in conclusion
Contrast transitions signal **contrasting or differing ideas.**	However, although, even though, nevertheless, on the other hand, but, in spite of, in contrast, instead, yet
Example transitions **help to show examples or illustrate ideas better.**	For example, for instance, including, such as, like

Argument Prewriting

When creating an argument essay, you should complete several prewriting strategies, such as free writing, listing, clustering, asking questions, outlining, and building a pyramid, to help you generate ideas. In addition to the above prewriting strategies, you may find a pro and con list helpful, especially if you plan to address the opposing viewpoints in your introduction or if you are unable to decide which stance would be easier to develop. If you get stuck while writing, you can return to the prewriting strategies or the pro and con list to generate additional ideas.

Argument Thesis Statement

The thesis statement states your topic, offers your stance, and provides three reasons that you will develop in the rest of your essay.

Argument Body Paragraphs

Each body paragraph begins with a topic sentence that states one of the three reasons listed in the thesis statement. Then, numerous supporting sentences follow. These supporting sentences, which consist of evidence, facts, observations, and examples, develop the topic and support your stance. A concluding sentence ends each body paragraph.

Conclusion Paragraph

The conclusion paragraph lets the reader know that the argument essay is coming to an end. You can use various techniques to end the essay. However, the call-to-action method is often used when writing argument essays.

Argument Outline

The format of an argument essay is the same as a standard five-paragraph essay. Below is a basic outline.

I.   Introduction
    a.   Introduction method
    b.   Thesis statement containing the three topics that will be developed

II. Body Paragraph 1
    a.   Topic sentence for main point 1
    b.   Supporting details—evidence, facts, observations, and examples
    c.   A concluding sentence

III. Body Paragraph 2
    a.   Topic sentence for main point 2
    b.   Supporting details—evidence, facts, observations, and examples
    c.   A concluding sentence

IV. Body Paragraph 3
    a.   Topic sentence for main point 3
    b.   Supporting details—evidence, facts, observations, and examples
    c.   A concluding sentence

V.   Conclusion
    a.   Thesis restatement
    b.   Conclusion method—call to action (optional)

ARGUMENT ESSAY EXAMPLE 1

Spare the Children

For several centuries, parents have thought that corporal punishment was a way to discipline children. During biblical times, people believed that it was a mandate from God to not spare disobedient children from harsh physical punishment. Proponents of spanking state that spanking children teaches them how to be respectful towards authority. Furthermore, some parents believe that because they were spanked as children that they should instill the same values into their own children. Granted, no one wants disobedient children, and some children who are spanked do change their negative behavior and refrain from repeating certain offenses; however, today there are healthier and more effective forms of discipline besides spanking. Most importantly there are negative consequences that result from spanking children. Parents should not spank their children because it causes emotional, mental, and physical harm.

First of all, when parents decide to spank their children, it could lead to emotional scarring. Children who are spanked will often hide their emotions inside, which will eventually lead to them acting out in some other way. For example, some children will become withdrawn and fearful of adults. Others, however, will release their pent up emotions violently by yelling and hitting other children who are smaller and weaker than they are. Another emotional consequence children who are spanked face is the tendency to become less likely to tell the truth when they get in trouble because they are afraid that they will be subjected to severe physical punishment. This emotional shortcoming sometimes leads to children growing up and becoming people pleasers instead of independent individuals who stand up for themselves. Additionally, children who are spanked often have feelings of self-worthlessness. They feel that they are not worthy of love because they cause their parents to get angry at them and spank them. Therefore, some children who are spanked feel that when they are faced with childhood issues they cannot go to their parents for comfort fearing they may be punished for voicing their feelings and opinions. Because of the emotional harm that spanking can cause, parents should never use it as a corrective choice.

Secondly, parents who spank their children are in danger of causing them to be harmed mentally. For example, some children who are spanked do not perform well in school. They are so concerned about giving the wrong answer in class that they do not enjoy learning. In their minds, wrong answers and mistakes lead to spankings. Consequently, their decision making and critical thinking skills are negatively affected. It is imperative that parents choose another method of discipline other than spanking so that children remain inquisitive beings who eagerly embrace new experiences and opportunities for learning.

Most importantly, spanking children damages them physically. Unfortunately, the TV news coverage bombards viewers with child abuse cases, each one more heartbreaking than the one before it. Some parents justify spanking their children so severely because that is the way that they were spanked when they were children. Many parents believe if a child's body is not covered with welts and bruises that the spanking was ineffective. Relying on what they were taught as children, some parents do not even know when the spanking should conclude; consequently, many children are left battered. Hospital emergency rooms are filled with children who have been spanked too severely. Doctors and nurses far too often have to get family services involved, which could lead to the destruction of the family unit—the placing of the child in foster care and the incarceration of the parent. Spanking children is detrimental to everyone involved.

The use of physical punishment as a means of discipline is ineffective. Spanking causes children to be emotionally harmed while they are children and when they enter adulthood. Furthermore, spanking affects children mentally by affecting their performance in school. The physical scarring that spanking yields is the cause of many children being taken away from their families. There is much to consider when it comes to disciplining children, and spanking should not be an option.

THINK *Write!*

Activity 11.4

Answer the following questions about "Spare the Children."

1. Underline the thesis statement.
2. Underline the three topic sentences. Circle the transitional devices.
3. Examine the first body paragraph about the emotional harm that spanking causes. What are some of its supporting points? _____

_____

_____

_____

_____

4. Examine the second body paragraph about the mental harm that spanking causes. What are some of its supporting points? _____

    _____

    _____

    _____

    _____

5. Examine the third body paragraph about the physical harm that spanking causes. What are some of its supporting points? _____

    _____

    _____

    _____

    _____

6. In the conclusion, is the thesis restatement the single sentence or the multisentence method?

    _____

ARGUMENT ESSAY EXAMPLE 2—
STUDENT ESSAY BY KIMBERLY RANDALL

Mandating Premarital Counseling

In the United States, half of all marriages end in divorce. Therefore, the odds of a marriage lasting "'til death do you part" are not in the couple's favor. However, marriage should be a happy union between two people that lasts forever. Although some people oppose the government becoming involved in personal matters, something must be done to increase the odds in favor of marriages lasting. Consequently, the government should pass a law that requires couples to go to premarital counseling before getting married because it would promote healthy marriages, lower the divorce rate, and decrease the number of children living in single-parent homes.

First, premarital counseling should be required to help promote healthy marriages. Marriage should be a healthy, positive union between two individuals who love and respect each other. However, some individuals end up getting married to someone they barely know to escape a bad home situation, for financial reasons, or for fear of being alone. Therefore, they may not know what a healthy relationship much less a healthy marriage is even supposed to look like, especially if they did not see one while they were growing up. Consequently, they are unaware that the key to a positive relationship is communication. Premarital counseling will teach couples how to know if they are compatible or not, how to talk to each other, how to really listen to one another, and how to disagree without being disagreeable. In premarital counseling, the engaged couple will also learn that a healthy marriage takes work, meaning time must be put into the marriage and that the "courting" it took to get the other person must continue throughout the marriage. For example, couples will learn about "date" night, ways to make time for one another, and little things to do to keep the marriage healthy, such as saying "I love you" and "good morning" daily. Having a healthy marriage takes work, but it is worth it.

Secondly, requiring couples to attend premarital counseling will lower the divorce rate. In today's society, marriages often fail, causing couples to end up in divorce court. Some issues that lead to divorce are financial problems, infidelity, disagreements involving the rearing of children, religious conflicts, or division of household chores. Whatever the issues are, people are not sticking around to work them out. Since the stigma of being divorced no longer exists, couples turn to divorce as their first option instead of their last. Premarital counseling would serve as a preventive divorce measure, meaning couples would learn the skills to work out these and other problems without fighting or ending the relationship.

Finally, passing a law requiring couples to go to premarital counseling will decrease the number of children living in single-parent homes. Although two-parent homes are no longer the norm, children who started with two parents benefit from having both of them. For example, girls learn how they are supposed to be treated by dates, and boys learn how to treat girls based on how they see their father treating their mother. If their parents end up getting a divorce, then the children lose out on having both parents in their lives on a daily basis. Furthermore, if the divorce is bitter, sometimes the children get dragged into the messy situation. For example, sometimes they have to choose which parent to live with or have their loyalty questioned by one or both of their parents. Worse of all, after a divorce, sometimes one of the parents abandons his/her children to escape having to have any contact with his/her ex-spouse. Children need to feel loved and nurtured by both of their parents instead of by just one of them in a single-parent home.

Marriage is supposed to be a beautiful institution, in which couples vow to stay together "for better or for worse" instead of ending the relationship at the very first sign of disharmony. In order to improve the odds of couples having stronger, longer lasting unions, the government should pass a law that requires couples to go to premarital counseling before getting married. The law would benefit everyone because premarital counseling would promote healthy marriages, the divorce rate would go down, and fewer children would have to live in single-parent homes. Concerned citizens must support the passing of this legislation because marriages are in jeopardy.

THINK  *Write!*

Activity 11.5

Answer the following questions about "Mandating Premarital Counseling."

1. Which kind of introduction method is used?
   a. A quote
   b. Surprising statement
   c. An anecdote
   d. General to specific
2. Underline the thesis.
3. How is the thesis statement made parallel?
   a. Each of the three points is expressed in a sentence within the thesis.
   b. Each of the three points begins with a phrase.
   c. Each of the three points begins with a verb.
4. Place an asterisk by the supporting points for the first body paragraph about promoting healthy marriages.

5. Place an asterisk by the supporting points for the second body paragraph about lowering the divorce rate.

6. Place an asterisk by the supporting points for the third body paragraph about decreasing the number of children living in single-parent homes.

7. How is the restatement of the thesis parallel?
   a. Each of the three points is expressed in a sentence within the restatement of the thesis.
   b. Each of the three points begins with a phrase.
   c. Each of the three points begins with a verb.

THINK Write!

Activity 11.6

On notebook paper, create a thesis and three topic sentences against requiring couples to go to premarital counseling.

THINK Write!

Activity 11.7

Fill in the missing information for the argument outline.

Thesis Statement

All eighteen year olds in the United States should not be required to complete one year of community service because they may have financial responsibilities, _____

_____

_____.

Body Paragraph 1

I. One reason teens should not be required to volunteer for a year is that they may have financial responsibilities.
    a. Help their parents out financially
    b. Have their own families to support
    c.
    d.

Body Paragraph 2

II. Another reason eighteen year olds should not have to volunteer is that _____

_____.

    a.
    b.
    c.
    d.

Body Paragraph 3

III.   The final reason teens should be exempt from volunteer service is that _____
_____ .

    a.

    b.

    c.

    d.

Argument Essay Topics

1. Should sex education classes be taught in middle school? High school?

2. Should colleges distribute free condoms?

3. Should concealed handguns be allowed on college campuses?

4. Should college professors date their students?

5. Should colleges enforce dress codes?

6. Should public school districts be able to fine parents for their children being truant?

7. Should ex-felons be able to vote?

8. Should gay and lesbian couples be allowed to adopt children?

9. Should corporal punishment be allowed in public school?

10. Should third trimester abortions be legal?

THINK *Write*/ Review Questions

1.   Why is it important to use tactful language?

2.   True/False   Arguments are always negative.

3.   What is a pro and con list?

4.   List two strategies for creating an introduction that acknowledges the opposing viewpoint.

5.   Which conclusion method is often used when writing an argument?

Chapter

Analysis Writing

Key Terms

Analyze, annotate, purpose, reading comprehension, critical thinking

Setting: an art gallery

Characters: Man 1 and Man 2

Man 1: "Hello, I see you are staring at this painting. What do you think of it?"

Man 2: "I think this painting is a piece of crap. I can't believe someone got paid for painting this. My three-year-old nephew could do a better job. It looks like the artist just threw some red paint on a canvas and stuck a bullet in the left side just for the heck of it."

Man 1: "Hmm, I see what you mean. But, when I painted it, I was trying to show the pain and bloodshed that war causes when a military regime runs a country instead of the people. I'll have to try to convey my message clearer next time."

Man 2: "Oh. Now that you've explained it to me I understand it better, but I still think it looks like a piece of crap."

When you **analyze** something, you go beyond the surface and take a closer look in order to gain a better understanding or appreciation. To critically examine something requires you to raise questions, to make judgments, and to be aware how prior knowledge and experiences affect your interpretation and understating. It is easier to analyze something once you have studied it and understand what you are being asked to analyze. When you are writing an analysis, it is important to do just that: analyze. When your professors ask you to write an analysis of a painting, a short story, a play, an essay, or a war, what they are asking you to do is to dissect or take apart the information you have been given, including any prior knowledge or biases you may have about the subject, study it again, and then put all the parts back together in order to gain a better understanding than you had before.

In this chapter, you are exposed to four professional writings. As you read the selections, you should **annotate**—jot down notes in the margins and circle, highlight, or underline key information or portions of the text that raise questions in your mind or stimulate your thinking. You will find that to delve deeper into a reading requires that you read it more than once; each time you read it you will discover something new, whether it is a clearer understanding of the author's tone, use of vocabulary, or **purpose**—the reason for writing.

At the end of each selection, there are questions and writing assignments to further assist you in strengthening your **reading comprehension**, your understanding of what you have read—and your **critical thinking** skills—the ability to actively think, discern, evaluate, and synthesize information. Critical thinking is a skill that you will need throughout your academic endeavors and in life as you make decisions regarding your career, your financial future, and your present situation.

Reading Selections

Reading 1

"Growing Up Bilingual" by Sara Gonzalez

Growing Up Bilingual

Sara Gonzalez

See instructor for reading.

Analysis Questions

1. What is the purpose of the first two paragraphs of this essay?

2. What is the main idea of this essay? Where is the main idea expressed?

3. How is dialogue used to enhance the narration?

4. What do you notice about the tone of this essay? Is it different than other essays you have read? Why or why not?

5. According to the principal and the teacher, what role should parents play in their children learning English? What do you think parents' roles should be? Do you believe parents should encourage their children to learn more than one language? Why or why not?

6. Do you think the mother should report the principal and the teacher to the school board? Why or why not?

7. Do you speak more than one language? What are the advantages? Any disadvantages?

8. The United States is one of the few countries in the world where people typically do not speak more than one language and where some companies mandate that employees speak only English even on breaks. What is your opinion on the following: Being bilingual? Bilingual education? Forbidding employees to speak their native language on breaks at work?

Writing Assignments

1. Write a narrative about a time when you experienced prejudice.

2. Create a brief dialogue between the principal and the teacher after the meeting ended. You will need to infer from what they said in the meeting to imagine what they would say after it. Make certain you incorporate their cultural prejudices.

3. Create a diary entry written by the mother about the incident that occurred. Include her disappointment, thoughts, feelings, and future hopes for her son.

Reading 2
"Fish Cheeks" by Amy Tan

Fish Cheeks

Amy Tan

1   I fell in love with the minister's son the winter I turned fourteen. He was not Chinese but as white as Mary in the manger. For Christmas, I prayed for this blond-haired boy, Robert, and a slim new American nose.

2   When I found out that my parents had invited the minister's family over for Christmas Eve dinner, I cried. What would Robert think of our shabby Chinese Christmas? What would he think of our noisy Chinese relatives who lacked proper American manners? What terrible disappointment would he feel upon seeing not a roasted turkey and sweet potatoes but Chinese food?

3   On Christmas Eve, I saw that my mother had outdone herself in creating a strange menu. She was pulling black veins out of the backs of fleshy prawns. The kitchen was littered with appalling mounds of raw food: a slimy rock cod with bulging eyes that pleaded not to be thrown into a pan of hot oil; tofu, which looked like stacked wedges of rubbery white sponges; a bowl soaking dried fungus back to life; and a plate of squid, their backs criss-crossed with knife markings so they resembled bicycle tires.

4   And then they arrived—the minister's family and all my relatives in a clamor of door-bells and rumpled Christmas packages. Robert grunted hello, and I pretended he was not worthy of existence.

5   Dinner threw me deeper into despair. My relatives licked the ends of their chopsticks and reached across the table, dipping them into the dozen or so plates of food. Robert and his family waited patiently for platters to be passed to them. My relatives murmured with pleasure when my mother brought out the whole steamed fish. Robert grimaced. Then my father poked his chopsticks just below the fish eye and plucked out the soft meat. "Amy, your favorite," he said, offering me the tender fish cheek. I wanted to disappear.

6   At the end of the meal, my father leaned back and belched loudly, thanking my mother for her fine cooking. "It's a polite Chinese custom to show you are satisfied," explained my father to our astonished guests. Robert was looking down at his plate with a reddened face. The minister managed to muster up a quiet burp. I was stunned into silence for the rest of the night.

7   After everyone had gone, my mother said to me, "You want to be the same as American girls on the outside." She handed me an early gift. It was a miniskirt in beige tweed. "But inside you must always be Chinese. You must be proud you are different. Your only shame is to have shame."

8   And even though I didn't agree with her then, I knew that she understood how much I had suffered during the evening's dinner. It wasn't until many years later—long after I had gotten over my crush on Robert—that I was able to fully appreciate her lesson and the true purpose behind our particular menu. For Christmas Eve that year, she had chosen all my favorite foods.

Analysis Questions

1. How does the author react when she realizes the boy she likes so much is coming to dinner?

2. The author's mother made a traditional Chinese meal. Discuss what you think was the reason for this. Discuss both the author's feelings and her mother's feelings toward Chinese customs and traditions.

3. Think about the different traditions and customs that are practiced. How does the author view her Chinese heritage as a teenager? How does she view her Chinese heritage as an adult?

4. How do you view your heritage? Has it changed as you have become older?

5. Discuss the author's purpose for writing "Fish Cheeks." Also, discuss the author's tone.

6. What do you believe the mother means when she says, "Your only shame is to have shame"?

Writing Assignments

1. Have the author write her mother a letter about the dinner experience now that the author as an adult understands the lesson her mother was trying to teach her.

2. Discuss a family tradition or a custom that you enjoy but that others might view as strange or different?

3. Write about a time in your childhood when you felt different? (Different could mean race, religion, gender, height, athletic ability, intelligence, etc.) How do you feel about the incident/situation now, looking back at it as an adult?

Reading 3
"Impounded Fathers" by Edwidge Danticat

Impounded Fathers

Edwidge Danticat

Please access reading at:
http://www.margueritelaurent.com/pressclips/danticat.html#fathers

Analysis Questions

1. Summarize or outline the essay according to the following grouping: Paragraphs 1 to 2, paragraphs 3 to 6, paragraphs 7 to 8, paragraph 9, paragraph 10, and paragraph 11.

2. What is the main idea of the essay? Where does Danticat state her thesis? Why do you think she waits until then to do so?

3. Discuss the significance of mentioning Father's Day in the first two paragraphs of the essay.

4. How do you think being separated from her father shaped Danticat's viewpoint on immigration?

5. Define impounded. What types of things come to mind when you hear that something has been impounded? Why do you think the author titles the essay "Impounded Fathers"?

6. Is Danticat's argument based more on emotion or logic? Do you think this strengthens or weakens her argument?

Writing Assignments

1. Write a one-page reading response to the essay addressing the following: What is your view on granting amnesty to law-abiding immigrants? What is your view on granting amnesty to immigrant parents who have American-born children? Does the fact that some people come to the United States seeking what everyone wants—a better life—affect your viewpoint in any way?

2. Write a letter to your father or the male figure in your life, regarding his role or lack of in your life.

Reading 4
"My Name" by Sandra Cisneros

My Name

Sandra Cisneros

In English my name means hope. In Spanish it means too many letters. It means sadness,   1
it means waiting. It is like the number nine. A muddy color. It is the Mexican records my
father plays on Sunday mornings when he is shaving, songs like sobbing.

It was my great-grandmother's name and now it is mine. She was a horse woman too,   2
born like me in the Chinese year of the horse—which is supposed to be bad luck if you're
born female—but I think this is a Chinese lie because the Chinese, like the Mexicans, don't
like their women strong.

My great-grandmother. I would've liked to have known her, a wild horse of a woman,   3
so wild she wouldn't marry. Until my great-grandfather threw a sack over her head and carried her off. Just like that, as if she were a fancy chandelier. That's the way he did it.
And the story goes she never forgave him. She looked out the window her whole life, the
way so many women sit their sadness on an elbow. I wonder if she made the best with
what she got or was she sorry because she couldn't be all the things she wanted to be.
Esperanza. I have inherited her name, but I don't want to inherit her place by the window.

At school they say my name funny as if the syllables were made out of tin and hurt the   4
roof of your mouth. But in Spanish my name is made out of a softer something, like
silver, not quite as thick as sister's name—Magdalena—which is uglier than mine. Magdalena who at least can come home and become Nenny. But I am always Esperanza.

I would like to baptize myself under a new name, a name more like the real me, the one   5
nobody sees. Esperanza as Lisandra or Maritza or Zeze the X. Yes. Something like Zeze the
X will do.

Analysis Questions

1. What literary terms are used to explain the meaning of Esperanza's name?
2. Why does the author give both the English and the Spanish meaning of her name?
3. How is Esperanza like her great-grandmother? How does she plan to be different from her ancestor?
4. Discuss the theme of female as second class citizen in "My Name."
5. What role do nick names play in "My Name"?
6. Why does Esperanza want to give herself a new name?

Writing Assignments

1.   Pretend you are a ten-year-old. Write Esperanza a letter sharing with her your views regarding her name, your thoughts regarding your own name—do you like it, dislike it, etc. Google your name and find out its meaning in several languages and include that as well.

2.   Read the selection below. Then, in an essay or a narrative, answer the following question: What is the story behind your name, one of your children's names, or a family member's name?

What's in a Name?

When my husband and I found out that we were going to be expecting a baby, we were so excited. After receiving the news we had been longing to hear for four years, we immediately began to start thinking about names. If we had a daughter, we agreed that her name would be Jasmine Nicole Alexander. I love the name Jasmine; it sounds so soothing to me. Jasmine is a fragrant flowering shrub and a pleasing perfume scent. Jasmine, our daughter, would be sweet and smart. Nicole is the name of our goddaughter who lives in Florida, and we both love her and the name. Perhaps, because we decided on a name for a girl so easily, we ended up having a boy. Agreeing upon a name for our son was very challenging.

My husband came to me one day and excitedly said, "Honey, I have the perfect name. If it is a boy, we will name him Michael Jordan."

I looked and him and said, "Sweetie, that name is taken."

Then, he said, "Okay, okay, how about Jordan Michael?"

I smiled and said, "Let's keep thinking. I'm sure that we can come up with just the right name that will make both of us happy and will not put any pressure on our child to be the world's best basketball player."

It would have been so easy if my husband wanted to name our son after himself. Unfortunately, my husband does not like his name, Brian Peter Raphael Alexander. My husband informed me, a Baptist by birth and a United Methodist by a marriage compromise, that it is a tradition in the Catholic faith to give one's child four names. He hates his first two names and only tolerates Raphael, so none of those names would do.

We decided to turn to baby books to find a name for our child that would be meaningful and acceptable to both of us. After three days, we agreed upon the perfect name for our son, Malik Elijah Alexander. In Arabic, Malik means king. Since my nickname is Queen Selena, giving our son a royal name was only fitting. His middle name, Elijah, represents two things very important to us. The first thing his middle name represents is our heritage. We chose the name Elijah to pay homage to Elijah Muhammad, the former leader of the black Muslims Movement in America; he taught and mentored Louis Farrakhan, the current leader of the black Muslims and the organizer of the Million Man March that my husband and I both attended in 1995. We also chose the name Elijah to represent our religious heritage. Elijah is one of the great prophets in the bible, known for his zeal for God.

Ever since our son was little, we have been telling him about the story behind his name. When we get to the part about his father wanting to name him Michael Jordan, he always laughs. Malik Elijah Alexander turned thirteen last week. As he goes through the challenging teen years, I am certain that my husband and I will be referring to the leadership and wisdom of Elijah Muhammad and the faith and praying power of the prophet Elijah to see us through until our Malik Elijah goes off to college.

THINK *Write!* **Review Questions**

1. Why is it important to analyze essays, paintings, poems, or literature?

2. Define annotating.

3. What is the purpose of annotating?

4. Why is it important to have good critical thinking skills?

PART III

The Mechanics Handbook

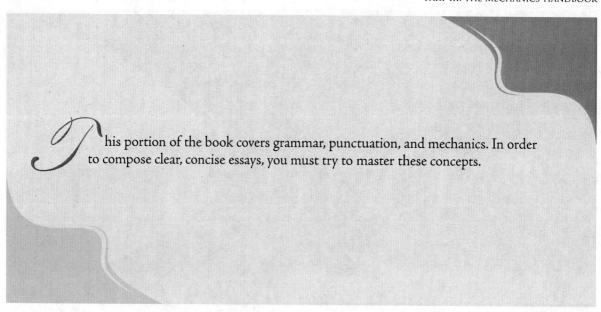

This portion of the book covers grammar, punctuation, and mechanics. In order to compose clear, concise essays, you must try to master these concepts.

Subjects and Verbs

Subjects and verbs are very important to developing sentence skills because they are what make up a complete sentence. Being able to identify and work with subjects and verbs is essential to smooth, polished writing that is easy to understand.

Subject

The subject of a sentence is who or what the sentence is about.

EXAMPLES

Carley is the head cheerleader.

The *picture* fell off the shelf.

That *cat* is always prowling around.

They are kind people.

Running is an excellent form of exercise.

THINK *Write!*

Activity 13.1

Circle the subject in the following sentences.

1. Alix is editor of the school newspaper.
2. It is an excellent publication.
3. Writing is something she really enjoys.
4. The staff loves working with her.
5. They work hard and get things done under her management.

Compound Subject

A compound subject is more than one subject in a sentence. A compound subject can be two, three, four, or more subjects in a sentence.

EXAMPLES

Carley and *Cynthia* are the head cheerleaders.

The *picture* fell off the shelf, and *it* shattered on the floor.

That *cat* is always prowling around, and our *dogs* often bark at it.

The *furniture, clothes, trunks,* and *boxes* have been put in the attic.

Napping, spending time with friends, and *playing computer games* are Melissa's spring break plans.

THINK *Write!*

Activity 13.2

Circle the compound subjects in the following sentences. Do not include conjunctions (for, and, nor, but, or, yet, so) as part of the subject.

1. Suzanne and Lucy are coming over to watch movies.
2. Dropping off the dry cleaning, picking up the prescription, and washing the car are on Andie's to do list today.
3. Helen and I want to go to the park this morning.
4. Parents and their children are both asked to sign the form.
5. Write a sentence below with a compound subject:

_____

_____

Verb

A verb is the action or state of being of the subject. It is what the subject is doing in a sentence (walk, talk, think, sing, etc.) or it links the subject to its state of being (is, are, was, were, am, be, being, seem, feel, have, like).

EXAMPLES

Carley *is* the head cheerleader.

The picture *fell* off the shelf.

That cat *is* always prowling around.

They *are* kind people.

Running *is* an excellent form of exercise.

THINK *Write!*

Activity 13.3

Underline the verb in the following sentences.

1.   The sunlight filtered through the dirty window.
2.   The door creaked slowly shut.
3.   The owl hooted in the deep of night.
4.   Those animals are always so noisy.
5.   The curtain opened up to reveal a small house set against a farm backdrop.

Compound Verb

A compound verb is more than one action of the subject in a sentence. There can be two or more verbs in a compound verb.

EXAMPLES

The old woman *was* bent over and *walked* slowly.

She *leaned* heavily on a cane and *limped* painfully.

A young man *came* over and *asked* her if she needed help crossing the street.

She *said* yes, *took* his arm, and *started* off with him.

THINK *Write!*

Activity 13.4

Underline the compound verbs in the following sentences.

1. The taco was greasy and fell apart when I picked it up.
2. The dog chased the Frisbee, caught it in its mouth, and ran back to its owner.
3. The baby tasted the lemon and then made a horrible face.
4. The cupcakes were frosted with pink icing and tasted absolutely delicious.
5. Write a sentence below with a compound verb:

_____

_____

_____

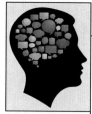 THINK *Write!*/TIP

There are actually two different definitions of "verb" in English. Although the two definitions are similar, they are not exactly the same.

> Verb: action or state of being (parts of speech)
>
> Verb: action of the subject (elements of the sentence)

When you are dealing with subjects, the "elements of the sentence" definition is the one that you need and what is covered in this chapter. The other definition is the general "parts of speech" definition. Sentences can have many verbs in them, but not all of those verbs are going to function as the action of the subject.

Verb Types

There are several different types of verbs in the English language. Identifying verbs is easier when you are aware of the different verb types.

Action Verb

An action verb is a word that shows true action, like "jump" or "dance." It is something that can actually be done. There are many action verbs in the English language.

EXAMPLES

Sean *programs* the computer.

The tree branches *swayed* gracefully in the wind.

Theeopal *danced* on the table.

Linking Verb

A linking verb is a word that connects a subject to its state of being. The most common linking verb is "be" and all its forms (am, is, are, was, were, being, been). Other verbs can function as linking verbs as well.

EXAMPLES

Scout *is* smart.

The office *was* a huge mess.

Oscar *became* happy when he found out he made the soccer team.

Paolo *grew* solemn when he heard the bad news.

Helping Verb

A helping verb is a verb type used to create verb tenses. The most common helping verbs are "have" and "be" and all their forms, although other verbs can also function as helping verbs. When you are asked to find the complete verb, it is necessary to include the helping verb as part of the action of the subject. This can make the verb two or even three words long. Always include the helping verb as well as the main verb when identifying complete verbs.

EXAMPLES

| helping verb(s) |
The pirate had buried his treasure on Sea Monkey Island.
| main verb |

| helping verb(s) |
Santa Monica Pier was built right on the Pacific Ocean.
| main verb |

| helping verb(s) |
The Lyrid meteor shower will be occurring after midnight tonight.
| main verb |

| helping verb(s) |
Sharnell has been taking dance lessons for 10 years.
| main verb |

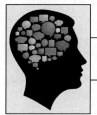 THINK *Write!* TIP

Helping verbs and their main verbs can also function as linking verbs. In the example above about Santa Monica Pier, "was built" is functioning as a linking verb.

THINK *Write!*

Activity 13.5

Circle the subject and underline the complete verb in the following sentences. Watch out for compound subjects and compound verbs.

1. The hand sanitizer has gotten lost in my purse.
2. Skiing in Colorado has been Kelisha's trip of choice since 2002.
3. Ethan will be attending SMU this fall.
4. Answering emails is going to be the priority today.
5. Write a sentence below using a helping verb with a main verb:

_____

_____

Things to Watch out For

When sentences get more complicated, it becomes more difficult to identify the subject and the verb. A few things you need to watch out for are the word *not*, prepositions, prepositional phrases, and infinitives.

Not

Not is not a verb. Therefore, it should not be included as part of the verb. It modifies the verb by making it negative, but when identifying verbs, do not include the word *not* as a part of the action of the subject.

EXAMPLES

Richard *was* not *planning* to attend the seminar.

William *is* not from California.

Raul *should* not *leave* his room for an hour.

The pants *were* not the right size.

The airplane *will* not *arrive* until later tonight.

Preposition

A preposition is a part of speech that shows relationships between nouns and pronouns. Many times, although not always, these are directional or location words. Below is a list of commonly used prepositions.

Commonly Used Prepositions			
about	above	across	after
along	among	around	as
at	before	behind	below
beneath	beside(s)	between	beyond
by	despite	down	during

except	for	from	in ✖
inside	into	near	of ✖
off	on	onto	out
outside	over	than	through
to	toward(s)	under	underneath
until	up	upon	with
within	without		

Prepositional Phrase

A prepositional phrase is a phrase that consists of a preposition, its object, and any words in between that connect them. Prepositional phrases usually take a three-word construction, but they can also be two, four, or more words.

EXAMPLES

Jumping *on the trampoline* can be good exercise.

The case *of trophies* is located in the front hall.

The house *by the car lot* is brand new.

Prepositional phrases can make it difficult to identify the subject. What is important to know is that **the subject is *not* found in a prepositional phrase** no matter how the sentence is put together. Therefore, to stay on track, cross out all prepositional phrases when looking for subjects and verbs. If you eliminate them, you will not be confused.

EXAMPLES

Jumping ~~*on the trampoline*~~ can be good exercise.

The case ~~*of trophies*~~ is located in the front hall.

The house ~~*by the car lot*~~ is brand new.

Once you have crossed out the prepositional phrases, the subjects of the above sentences quickly become clear: "jumping," "case," and "house." The words "trampoline" "trophies," and "car lot" are no longer confusing because they have been eliminated.

THINK  *Write!*

Activity 13.6

Cross out all prepositional phrases in the following sentences.

1. The door to the office is jammed in its frame, making it impossible to get in to retrieve the students' graded tests.
2. Each of the students wanted to be "teacher" for the day and stand up at the front of the classroom and lecture.

3. One of my shoes fell off into the mud puddle, ruining it for future use.
4. The twinkle lights in the trees shone brightly from above, sparkling like stars in the night sky.
5. Write a sentence below with a prepositional phrase in it:

_____

_____

_____

Infinitive

An infinitive is a verbal created by "to + a verb." Examples include to run, to jump, and to play. Any verb with the word "to" in front of it becomes an infinitive.

Infinitives can make it difficult to properly identify verbs because they look very similar to verbs. However, they are not verbs but verbals—verb forms that function as nouns or modifiers instead of verbs in a sentence. Infinitives cannot function as the action of the subject in a sentence. You will find it helpful to cross out infinitives as well as prepositional phrases.

EXAMPLES

Vivienne *has gone* ~~to pick up~~ her son from daycare.

Erin *is going* ~~to attend~~ college this fall.

Ronald *wants* ~~to sled~~ down the hill after school.

THINK *Write!*

Activity 13.7

Cross out any infinitives *and* prepositional phrases you see in the following sentences.

1. All of the students danced the Macarena to relieve stress before finals.
2. The announcer shouted into the microphone to get the crowd revved up.
3. The journalist asked questions to gather information for the story and to check facts.
4. Jordan walked to the bus stop to catch a ride to work.
5. Write a sentence below with an infinitive in it:

_____

_____

_____

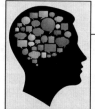

THINK *Write!* TIP

The first step to always take when asked to identify subjects and verbs is to cross out prepositional phrases and infinitives. Then, look for either the subject or the verb. However, if you find it difficult to identify the subject, identify the verb first. Then, it usually becomes clear who or what is doing the action.

will reverse the order of the subject and the verb. Sentences that begin with "here" or "there" can also reverse the subject and verb order. It is possible to reverse this order other ways as well, just depending on how the sentence is constructed.

EXAMPLES

Do <u>you</u> *like* that Enrique Iglesias song?

Where *is* the <u>newspaper</u> this morning?

Here *is* today's <u>edition</u> under the car.

There *is* the <u>one</u> from yesterday, as well.

In the bushes *is* last week's <u>edition</u>.

THINK *Write!*

Activity 14.3

The following sentences have the subjects and the verbs reversed. Cross out any prepositional phrases. Then, choose the correct verb form to go with the subject.

1. Under the tree (is/are) so many Christmas presents.
2. There (is/are) a shop down on Main Street that sells custom tee shirts.
3. Down on the corner (is/are) a lemonade stand where passersby can get a drink for a quarter.
4. (Is/Are) Polly and Grace hosting their annual charity event this year?
5. (Has/Have) Sherry made her famous caramel cake for dessert?

Working with Compound Subjects

Compound subjects also make it difficult to ensure subjects and verbs agree. Compound subjects are either joined by the conjunction *and* or the conjunction *or*.

Compound subjects joined by *and* are considered plural. They will always take a plural verb.

EXAMPLES

Running and skiing are Daniel's favorite leisure activities.

The car and the boat were parked in the driveway.

Compound subjects joined by *or* are considered singular or plural, depending on the subjects. If both of the compound subjects are singular, the verb will be singular, as in the examples below.

EXAMPLES

Running or skiing is Daniel's favorite leisure activity.

The car or the boat was parked in the driveway.

If both of the subjects are plural, the verb will be plural, as in the examples below.

EXAMPLES

The moms or the dads pick up the children from school.

The lions or the tigers eat all the meat.

Difficulty occurs if the compound subject is comprised of a singular subject and a plural subject. When this occurs, match the verb to the subject sitting closest to it in the sentence.

EXAMPLES

The breadsticks or the salad comes with the meal.

In the first example, salad, which is singular, is closest to the verb. Therefore, the singular verb "comes" goes with it.

The salad or the breadsticks come with the meal.

In the second example, breadsticks, which is plural, is closest to the verb. Therefore, the plural verb "come" goes with it.

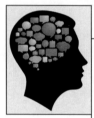

THINK *Write!* / TIP

Subject–verb agreement can get confusing because it is the opposite of what you are used to thinking. When an "s" is added to a noun, it makes the noun plural. However, if an "s" is added to a present tense verb, it makes it third person singular. This can get baffling, so one way to keep from getting confused is to remember this: if the subject has an "s" on it, then the verb usually will not have an "s" on it. Keep in mind, however, that some words, like class and recess, already end in "s" but are considered singular. For these kinds of words, the trick above cannot be used; instead read and choose the verb form carefully.

THINK *Write!*

Activity 14.4

Choose the correct verb form for the following compound subjects. Be aware of which conjunction is connecting the compound subjects and do not forget to cross out prepositional phrases.

1. The horse and its rider (races/race) across the finish line.
2. The puppy or the kitten (is/are) always napping in the sun by the window.
3. Pencils or a pen (is/are) needed for the test tomorrow.
4. Roger or Josie (has/have) the money we need.
5. The shelf or the floor lamps (needs/need) to be put into storage.

Chapter 15

Sentence Patterns

Look up for Commonly confused words eg → Loose and Lost

Sentence patterns create sentence variety and engage the reader. If every sentence in your essay was a simple sentence, your writing would be choppy and boring. There are four sentence patterns to use to create sentence variety.

Simple Sentences

A simple sentence is the basic sentence form; it is a single independent clause. It stands on its own and expresses one idea. It can have one subject and one verb, or it can contain compound subjects and/or compound verbs.

EXAMPLES

The telephone rang continuously all afternoon.

Nicole got a job at the casino and rose through the ranks to a high paying position.

Chan and Lewis decided to dress as a horse for Halloween.

Sophie loves to chase the laser pointer.

THINK *Write!*

Activity 15.1

Write five simple sentences on the lines below.

1. _____
2. _____
3. _____
4. _____
5. _____

Compound Sentences

Compound sentences contain two or more independent clauses and are created using coordination. There are two ways to coordinate ideas and create compound sentences.

Comma and a Coordinating Conjunction

Independent clauses can be combined by joining them with a comma and a coordinating conjunction. There are seven coordinating conjunctions, and you can memorize them by using the acronym FAN-BOYS. The meaning of each of the coordinating conjunctions is discussed more in Chapter 17: Run-ons and Comma Splices.

F	For
A	And
N	Nor
B	But
O	Or
Y	Yet
S	So

Compound sentences using the FANBOYS have a subject and a verb on either side of the comma and the coordinating conjunctions.

EXAMPLES

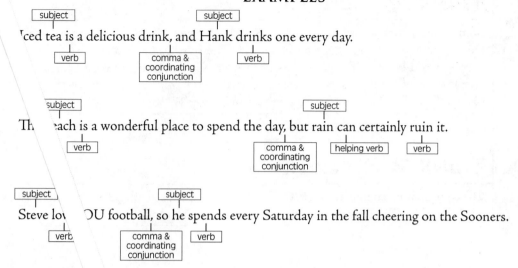

Iced tea is a delicious drink, and Hank drinks one every day.

The beach is a wonderful place to spend the day, but rain can certainly ruin it.

Steve loves OU football, so he spends every Saturday in the fall cheering on the Sooners.

THINK *Write!*

Activity 15.2

Write five compound sentences using a comma and one of the FANBOYS on the lines below. Try to use different FANBOYS each time.

1. _____
2. _____
3. _____
4. _____
5. _____

Semicolon

A semicolon can also be used to create compound sentences. Use it to combine two independent clauses that go together by simply placing the semicolon at the end of the first clause. Do not capitalize the first letter of the second clause.

EXAMPLES

The snow is getting so deep; we will have to shovel the walk tomorrow.

Macbeth is my favorite Shakespeare play; I love the witches' chants.

Meredith needs a new car; therefore, she will head to the car lot this weekend.

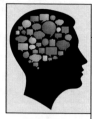

THINK *Write!*/TIP

Sometimes it is necessary to use a connecting word after the semicolon to help the sentences being joined come together smoothly. The third example above has such a connecting word because "therefore" has been used. Conjunctive adverbs (transitional devices) work well for this purpose, such as *therefore, consequently, however,* and *also.* Conjunctive adverbs are discussed further in Chapter 17: Run-ons and Comma Splices.

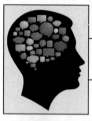

THINK *Write!*/TIP

The coordinating conjunctions (FANBOYS) cannot be used after the semicolon. To use one of the FANBOYS, put a comma in front of it, not a semicolon.

THINK *Write!*

Activity 15.3

Write five compound sentences using semicolons on the lines below. For at least two, try to use a connecting word after the semicolon, such as *therefore, consequently,* or *however.*

1. _____

2. _____

3. _____

4. _____

5. _____

Complex Sentences

A complex sentence has two parts: an independent clause and a dependent clause. Independent clauses are complete sentences that can stand on their own; they have a subject, a verb, and they express a complete thought. Dependent clauses rely on independent clauses to make sense. Even though they may look as though they have a subject and a verb, they do not express a complete thought. This is because they contain subordinating conjunctions.

Subordinating Conjunctions

Subordinating conjunctions are dependent words, like *because, since,* or *when.* When these kinds of words are added to a sentence, they create dependent clauses.

EXAMPLES

dependent clause   independent clause

Because I did my homework, I made a good grade on the test.

independent clause   dependent clause

I was surprised to find a package on the doorstep when I got home.

independent clause   dependent clause

I will watch television tonight if I finish reading my textbook by eight.

In the examples above, "because I did my homework," "when I got home," and "if I finish reading my textbook by eight" are the dependent clauses because they cannot stand on their own. If the independent clauses are taken away, incomplete thoughts are left, which are sentence fragments.

There are many subordinating conjunctions to use to create complex sentences. Below is a list of the common ones. Remember, however, that there are many more.

Common Subordinating Conjunctions			
after	before	once	although
as	as long as	as though	because
even if	even though	if	now that
rather than	since	unless	until
when	whenever	where	wherever
while			

Some of the most common subordinating conjunctions are discussed further in Chapter 17: Run-ons and Comma Splices.

Complex sentences can be put together two ways: begin the sentence with the dependent clause or end it with the dependent clause. If the dependent clause starts the sentence, use a comma before the independent clause begins because the dependent clause is considered introductory.

EXAMPLES

If Melanie goes to the Halloween party, she will need a costume.

When the tree blew over, it fell on Edwin's car.

Although I like cake, I prefer ice cream.

These same sentences can be more or less reversed. If the dependent clause comes at the end of the complex sentence, no comma is needed.

EXAMPLES

Melanie will need a costume *if she goes to the Halloween party.*

The tree fell on Edwin's car *when the tree blew over.*

I prefer ice cream *although I like cake.*

THINK *Write!*

Activity 15.4

Write six complex sentences on the lines below. For three, put the dependent clause first. For the other three, put the dependent clause second.

1. _____
2. _____
3. _____
4. _____
5. _____
6. _____

Compound–Complex Sentences

Compound–complex sentences contain two independent clauses, like a compound sentence, and a dependent clause, like a complex sentence.

EXAMPLES

Ann traveled to Malaysia; while she was away, her daughter's apartment was burglarized.

Although the weather is sunny right now, it is supposed to rain later, so I brought my umbrella.

The chorus book was expensive to purchase, but Nellie had the money because she had just gotten paid.

It is possible to put compound–complex sentences together several ways. The dependent clause and independent clauses can be put together whichever way you prefer or whichever way sounds best.

THINK *Write!*

Activity 15.5

Write five compound–complex sentences on the lines below. Try to use several different methods to put the sentences together by sometimes putting the dependent clause first, in the middle, or last.

1. _____
2. _____
3. _____
4. _____
5. _____

Chapter 15 Review Exercise

Identify the types of sentences in the paragraph below. Write "simple" above simple sentences, "compound" above compound sentences, "complex" above complex sentences, and "compound–complex" over compound–complex sentences. There are seven simple sentences, two compound sentences, two complex sentences, and two compound–complex sentences.

Chores! Chores! Chores!

Chores are a vital part of maintaining a clean household. Three of the most important chores to complete are doing the dishes, doing the laundry, and taking out the trash. First, doing the dishes is imperative. They should really be done after every meal. If they do not get done in a timely manner, they pile up, and this can get really disgusting. Next, it is essential to do the laundry. Doing the laundry ensures everyone in the house has clean clothes, and no one has to worry about smelling bad because their clothes have not been washed. Also, this keeps clothes from piling up on the floor, so people will not trip over them. The last significant chore is taking out the trash. Trash needs to be taken out often because it can get smelly. It also has bacteria in it, and it can make people sick. Trash needs to be removed from the house promptly. When it comes to chores, doing the dishes, doing the laundry, and taking out the trash are the most important ones.

Sentence Fragments

Complete sentences are key to polished writing. Complete sentences allow for understanding, but fragments can make it hard for the reader to comprehend the message you are trying to get across.

Sentence Fragment

A sentence fragment is an incomplete sentence. It is missing something. A complete sentence is made up of a subject, a verb, and a complete thought—all of which are discussed in depth in Chapter 13: Subjects and Verbs. When one of these parts is missing, a fragment occurs. Sentence fragments cannot stand by themselves. There are four different types of sentence fragments listed below.

Missing Piece Fragment

A missing piece fragment occurs when a key part of a sentence is missing, like a subject or a verb.

EXAMPLES

The movers loading everything into the truck.

Is so tiring to watch.

Dependent Clause Fragments

Dependent clause fragments occur when a dependent clause has been separated from an independent clause it should be attached to.

EXAMPLES

Because it is past midnight. Kevin is going to bed.

All of the spectators left their seats and ran into the stadium. *After it started to rain.*

Example and Exception Fragments

Example and exception fragments occur when words and phrases like "for example," "for instance," "like," "such as," "with," "except," and "without" are used.

EXAMPLES

Brian has many hobbies. For example, bird watching.

I want so many rooms in my dream house. Like a library, a conservatory, a dining room, a gym, and a bowling alley.

Verbal Fragments

Verbal fragments occur when a writer has accidently used a verbal instead of a verb in the sentence. There are three types of verbals.

- Infinitives: to + a verb
  To prepare *for the marathon.* Allison ran every day after work.

- Gerunds: verb + ing
  Maribeth ran down the street. **Singing** *at the top of her lungs.*

- Participle: past tense/participle form of the verb
  No one saw the hidden recording device. **Tucked** *away in Elmer's pocket.*

Below are steps you can take to identify sentence fragments.

Step 1: Identify the subject of the sentence; if there is not one, it is a fragment.

THINK  *Write!*

Activity 16.1

Write the subjects of the following sentences on the lines preceding them. If there is not one, put an "F" for fragment instead.

1. _Jim_ Jim took a trip down to Cancun, Mexico.
2. _____ Rode all the way there in the back of a truck.
3. _____ The trip itself was wonderful, and Jim enjoyed himself.

4. _____ Once in Mexico, spent every day at the beach.
5. _____ Was hot.
6. _____ To keep cool.
7. _____ Jim decided to stay in the shade.
8. _____ And drink cool drinks to stay hydrated.
9. _____ Like water and coconut juice.
10. _____ The trip was absolutely fabulous.

Step 2: If the sentence appears to have a subject, find the verb that goes with that subject; if the subject is not completing an action or in a state of being, it is a fragment.

THINK 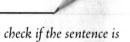 *Write!*

Activity 16.2

Underline the subjects in the following sentences. Then, write the verbs of the subjects on the lines preceding them. If there is not a subject, put an "F" for fragment instead. Watch out for compound verbs and prepositional phrases.

1. _____ The wedding was very beautiful.
2. _____ Everyone standing when the bride came in.
3. _____ At the reception.
4. _____ Sandra caught the bouquet.
5. _____ After shoving Sabrina down and jumping really high.

Step 3: If it appears as though the sentence has a subject and a verb, the last thing to do is check if the sentence is a complete thought. If it stops abruptly, it is a fragment. A good way to test this is to read the sentence aloud.

THINK *Write!*

Activity 16.3

Determine whether the following sentences are complete thoughts or not. If they are, put a "C" for correct on the line preceding them. If they are not, put an "F" for fragment.

1. _____ Boy bands were very popular in the late 1990s.
2. _____ Especially Backstreet Boys and NSYNC.
3. _____ Both groups toured extensively and had platinum records.
4. _____ However, before boy bands were popular.
5. _____ Grunge music ruled the radio.

THINK *Write!*

Activity 16.4

Read the sentences below. If the sentence is correct, put a "C" for correct on the line preceding it. If it is a fragment, put an "F."

1. _____ Driving to Alaska.
2. _____ Is a long trip but an exciting experience.
3. _____ Driving the short way only takes two weeks.
4. _____ However, travelers miss out on the Grand Canyon and Disneyland.
5. _____ The long way can take a month.
6. _____ Because there are so many ways to go.
7. _____ Whichever way they decide to drive.
8. _____ Travelers can see San Francisco, Seattle, and parts of Canada.
9. _____ For instance, British Columbia and the Yukon Territory.
10. _____ The Alcan Highway is the way to go by car.

When asked to identify fragments, follow all three steps with every sentence being scrutinized. If one or more of the three pieces is missing, it is a fragment.

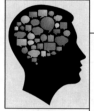

THINK *Write!*/TIP

Generally speaking, a sentence that starts with the word "which" is going to be a fragment. The only exception to this is if the sentence is a question.

Fragment: Which is on the way to the museum.

Not a fragment: Which way is the museum?

Correcting Fragments

There are two ways to correct fragments: add words, like a subject or a verb, or connect the fragment to a nearby sentence that it makes sense with. It is not really possible to use these correction methods interchangeably. Look at each fragment individually and make the best correction for it. Some will obviously need to be connected to nearby sentences because they never should have been separated from the nearby sentence in the first place, like dependent clause fragments, verbal fragments, and some example/exception fragments. Others will need a subject or a verb added to easily make the correction, like missing piece fragments and some example/exception fragments.

EXAMPLES

Jose walking the dog. Later went to pick up his dry cleaning. And then out to dinner.

The first sentence needs a verb added: Jose *was* walking the dog, or you could change walking to the past tense walked.

The second sentence needs a subject added: Later *he* went to pick up his dry cleaning.

The third sentence should be connected to the second sentence: Later *he* went to pick up his dry cleaning and then out to dinner.

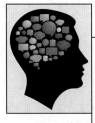 THINK *Write*/TIP

> The coordinating conjunctions (FANBOYS) should almost *never* start sentences. Although professional writers, like journalists and novelists, are known to start sentences with coordinating conjunctions, it should not be done in formal, academic writing for school. They are used to connect two sentences, so the FANBOYS go in the middle of sentences.
>
> Wrong: The recital began. *And the dancer leapt into the air.*
> Correct: The recital began, and the dancer leapt into the air.
>
> Wrong: The flight could come in today. *Or it could be delayed until tomorrow.*
> Correct: The flight could come in today, or it could be delayed until tomorrow.
>
> Wrong: I did not want to go to the party. *But Denise wanted to go.*
> Correct: I did not want to go to the party, but Denise wanted to go.

Only one of the FANBOYS is an exception to this rule, and that is "so" when it is functioning as an adverb and not a conjunction.

EXAMPLE

So far I have gotten juice and pretzels.

In this sentence, "so" is being used as an adverb to modify the word "far" and not as a coordinating conjunction.

For Example and For Instance: The Exceptions to the Connection Rule

"For example" and "for instance" often create fragments. When correcting fragments with "for example" and "for instance" in them, do not connect them to the sentence that comes before them. Instead, add words to create a new sentence beginning with "for example" or "for instance."

EXAMPLES

Buddy has many toys. For example, tennis balls, Kongs, and chew ropes.

Although it is tempting, you cannot connect the "for example" sentence to the part about Buddy. In this instance, words must be added to create a complete sentence, like the examples below.

🐾 Buddy has many toys. For example, tennis balls, Kongs, and chew ropes *are in his toy basket.*

🐾 Buddy has many toys. For example, *he has* tennis balls, Kongs, and chew ropes.

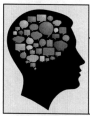

THINK *Write!*/TIP

When correcting fragments, do not be afraid to add or take away words as needed to help the sentence make sense. The only thing that should not be done is changing the meaning of the sentence.

THINK *Write!*

Activity 16.5

Underline the five fragments in the following paragraph. Then, make corrections by adding words or connecting the fragments to nearby sentences they make sense with. Write your corrections in between the lines.

Oliver: A Future Writer

When Oliver grows up. He wants to be a writer. Every day he practices writing. Even though he is only four. To improve his penmanship. He writes the alphabet several times a day. Is very time consuming. But he loves it. Someday he will be a great writer.

THINK *Write!*

Activity 16.6

Underline the five fragments in the following paragraph. Then, make corrections by adding words or connecting the fragments to nearby sentences they make sense with. Write your corrections in between the lines.

Water Park Fun

The water park is the most fun place to go in the summer. First, the lazy river. It is relaxing to get an inner tube and float around all day in the sun. Whole groups can hold hands. And drift around together. Next, the wave pool is amusing. People can ride the waves on inner tubes or stay in the shallow end and float on their own. Staying in the wave pool all day can make people feel like they are still in the pool. Even when they are not. Finally, the slides. They are the best. It is so fun to go blasting down through the water. Like a roller coaster. Everyone should go to the water park this summer.

Chapter 16 Review Exercise

Underline the sentence fragments in the following paragraph. Then, make corrections by either adding words or connecting the fragments to nearby sentences. Write your corrections in between the lines. There are ten errors.

The Odd, Old House

When I was a little girl. I lived in an old house that was really weird. It had been built in the 1940s. And originally had just been a three-room log cabin with a basement. Over the years, rooms and stories added. Giving the house a peculiar look. The original part of the house made of huge, varnished spruce tree logs, and the rest of the house was made of unpainted wood siding. Inside was just as strange. A handmade, wooden spiral staircase led down into the newer basement. The older basement had a narrow, rickety staircase that ended near an old, closed up well. Upstairs, the original bedroom, now used for a study, always seemed to be cast in darkness. Going in there gave anyone a chill down his/her spine; there was something creepy about that room. Upstairs were two more bedrooms. Neither room had a closet; instead, there was one in the hallway. My brother and I sharing it. Also, in the hallway was a random door on the side of the house. Since it was on the second story. It opened up over the tin roof of the mudroom. Which no one could walk on because it was not meant to support weight. We called that door the "door to nowhere." Because no one could actually use it. So random. In fact, the whole house was very odd; my dad was convinced it was haunted, and I am not sure he was wrong. We moved out after only a year.

Chapter 17

Run-Ons and Comma Splices

Two sentence errors that you must be on the lookout for and avoid are run-ons and comma splices.

A **run-on** sentence occurs when two or more complete sentences (independent clauses) are joined together with no punctuation between them.

    Julius has been reviewing his biology notes he is ready for the final exam.

A **comma splice** occurs when two complete sentences (independent clauses) are improperly joined with just a comma. In other words, a comma is trying to be a period or a semicolon.

    Julius has been reviewing his biology notes, he is ready for the final exam.

As you look for run-ons and comma splices, you must ask yourself the following important question: ***Can I put a period somewhere and make two separate sentences?*** If the answer is yes, then the sentence is a run-on or a comma splice.

Ask the question for the sentence below: ***Can I put a period somewhere and make two separate sentences?***

    The python slithered through the swamp it was seeking its dinner.

The answer is yes; the sentence is a run-on. A period can be placed after swamp.

    The python slithered through the swamp. It was seeking its dinner.

What about the sentence below? ***Can I put a period somewhere and make two separate sentences?***

✍ The band members were drunk and loud.

The answer is no. *The band members were drunk* is a sentence, but *and loud* is NOT a sentence. Therefore, the sentence must stay altogether.

Try one more. ***Can I put a period somewhere and make two separate sentences?***

✍ My watch needs a new battery, it keeps losing 10 minutes every day.

The answer is yes; the sentence is a comma splice. The comma needs to be replaced with a period.

✍ My watch needs a new battery. It keeps losing 10 minutes every day.

Although inserting a period is not the only way to correct run-ons and comma splices, it is the question to ask as you analyze each of your sentences to determine whether it is a run-on or a comma splice.

Four Ways to Correct Run-Ons and Comma Splices

1. Make two separate sentences using a period.
    ✍ Julius has been reviewing his biology notes. He is ready for the final exam.

2. Connect using a semicolon by itself or a semicolon, a conjunctive adverb (transition), and a comma.
    ;   ; therefore,   ; however,   ; furthermore,   ; then,
             ; consequently,   ; nevertheless,   ; moreover,
             ; thus,   ; in addition,
    ✍ Julius has been reviewing his biology notes; he is ready for the final exam.
    ✍ Julius has been reviewing his biology notes; **therefore,** he is ready for the final exam.

3. Connect using a comma and one of the coordinating conjunctions (FANBOYS):
    , for
    , and
    , nor
    , but
    , or
    , yet
    , so
    The comma goes in front of the conjunction and follows this pattern:
    a complete sentence + comma and one of the FANBOYS + a complete sentence
    ✍ Julius has been reviewing his biology notes, so he is ready for the final exam.

4. Connect using a subordinating conjunction.
    because   although   before   if   where   when   until
    since   even though   after   as if   whereas   whenever   unless
    so that   though   while   as   wherever   while
    ✍ **Because** Julius has been reviewing his biology notes, he is ready for the final exam.
    ✍ Julius is ready for the final exam **because** he has been reviewing his notes.

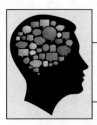

THINK *Write!*/TIP

Notice that subordinating conjunctions can be placed at the beginning of the sentence or in the middle of the sentence. When the subordinating conjunction begins the sentence, never put a comma right after it; the comma goes where the dependent clause ends.

THINK *Write!*

Activity 17.1

Determine whether the following sentences are correct or not. If the sentence is correct, put a "C" on the line preceding it. If the sentence is not, put an "RO" for run-on or a "CS" for comma splice. Four sentences are correct.

1. _RO_ The music was blaring from the radio Ricardo could not fall asleep.
2. _CS_ The music was blaring from the radio, Ricardo could not fall asleep.
3. _CS_ Because the music was blaring from the radio, Ricardo could not fall asleep.
4. _CS_ I hate going to the grocery store, the lines are always long.
5. _C_ I try to go through the twenty items or less lane, but I usually have twenty-four items.
6. _C_ Vanessa's roses are gorgeous she should enter them in a contest.
7. _C_ Her roses look so lovely because she takes the time to cultivate them.
8. _RO_ Marco jogs ten miles every day he plans to run a marathon next fall.
9. _C_ The forecast calls for clear skies and warm weather.
10. _RO_ The gift card had $22 left on it, Jerome plans to buy a new dress shirt.

THINK *Write!*

Activity 17.2

The following paragraph has five run-ons and five comma splices in it. Correct the paragraph by adding periods and capital letters as needed.

A Life-Changing Event

Last night my life changed. I won the lottery. The jackpot was $16 million, I could not believe my good fortune. I immediately called my parents. They were very happy and excited for me. Then, I called my girlfriend, she screamed for joy in my ear for five minutes. After she calmed down, she asked me what I was going to do with the money. I had no idea; I never expected to win. After thinking about it for a few minutes, I decided on a few things to do. First, I would buy a new car my Ford truck has over 200,000 miles on it. I decided on a red Hummer. Since I had just won a huge amount of money, I was not worried about high gas prices I figured that I had enough money now to buy my own gas station. Next, I decided to buy a ranch for my parents in Billings, Montana, I knew that would make them very

152   PART III: THE MECHANICS HANDBOOK

happy. Plus, it would give me a place to visit in the summer and winter. For my brother, I decided to take him on an all-expense paid vacation to Puerto Rico, he has always wanted to go there. He says the island is beautiful it offers so much to see and do. For example, we can be in the mountains one minute, in the rain forest the next, and on the beach in the evening. We are going to have a fantastic trip I will purchase a new video camera to record our good times. I have decided to propose to my girlfriend on Valentine's Day, then, we will plan a spectacular wedding of her dreams. I am not going to tell her about my plans. All I told her was that I was going to buy her some jewelry. Winning the lottery has changed my life I just hope that money does not change me.

Chart of the Seven Coordinating Conjunctions (FANBOYS)

Coordinating Conjunction	Meaning	Example Sentence
, for	Because, shows cause	The pen did not work, *for* it was out of ink.
, and	Shows addition	The reality show is a hit, *and* it continues to attract new viewers.
, nor	Not either one	The babysitter did not answer the house phone, *nor* did he answer his cell phone.
, but	Contrast	Lisa loves to shop, *but* she only buys items on sale.
, or	Provides an alternative or choice/option	Blake will vacation in San Antonio in the summer, *or* he will go to Denver in the winter.
, yet	Contrast	The white board was brand new, *yet* it would not erase like the old one.
, so	As a result, shows effect	Ling makes the best apple pie, *so* she wins the dessert contest every year.

THINK *Write!*

Activity 17.3

Determine whether the following sentences are run-ons or comma splices. If they are run-ons, put an "RO" on the line preceding them. If they are comma splices, put a "CS."

Then, correct the run-ons or the comma splice by adding a comma and a coordinating conjunction (FANBOYS).

Example

                                                                     and

   CS Lamont enjoys playing hockey, ∧ he enjoys watching wrestling.

1. _____ The pony is very gentle little kids like to ride it.

2. _____ The wedding cost over $50,000 the bride wore a Vera Wang gown.

3. _____ Lionel Richie used to be a member of the Commodores, now he is a solo act.

4. _____ The sky was perfectly clear the forecast called for rain.

5. _____ The judge banged on her gavel, the trial began.

THINK *Write!*

Activity 17.4

Combine the following run-ons using a semicolon.

Example

$$;$$

The toddler took his first step ∧ his parents clapped their hands with joy.

1. Gabriel enjoys playing hockey he hopes to play in the National Hockey League one day.
2. One of Gabriel's heroes is Wayne Gretzky he is considered the greatest hockey player of all time.
3. Gretzky's father built an ice skating rink in the family's backyard as a boy, Gretzky would practice for hours on end.
4. Wayne Gretzky began his professional hockey career in Canada then, he played in the United States on several teams.
5. The NHL retired Gretzky's number, which is 99 this is an honor only a few athletes receive.

Chart of Most Frequently Used Conjunctive Adverbs (Transitions)

Transition	Meaning	Example Sentence
Therefore,	As a result	Julia is very friendly; therefore, she has numerous friends.
Consequently,	As a result	I studied for the exam; consequently, I made an A on it.
However,	Contrast	I want to lose weight, however, I do not make the time to exercise.
Nevertheless,	Contrast	Angel's leg has been bothering him; nevertheless, he is determined to participate in the walkathon.
Furthermore,	Shows addition	The tornado destroyed houses; furthermore, it uprooted trees.

THINK *Write!*

Activity 17.5

Correct the run-ons by filling in the blank with a semicolon, a transitional word, and a comma. Try not to use the same transitional word more than once.

Example

Karen loves cats ____**; however,**____ her husband is allergic to them.

1. One of Vanessa's favorite television shows is *America's Next Top Model* _____ she tunes in to watch it every week.
2. Tyra Banks, a former supermodel, is the show's creator, host, and head judge _____ she serves as the show's co-executive producer.
3. On the reality show, which debuted in May 2003, the young ladies compete for a modeling contract and other prizes _____ thousands of contestants send in audition tapes every year.
4. At times, the model hopefuls have to pose in frightful situations, such as with reptiles, in the air, or underwater in tanks _____ they are expected to take great pictures.

Chart of Most Frequently Used Subordinating Conjunctions

Subordinating Conjunction	Meaning	Example Sentence
Although	Contrast	*Although* I want to lose weight, I do not make the time to exercise.
		I do not make the time to exercise *although* I want to lose weight.
Even though	Contrast	*Even though* Morgan apologized three times, Lilly will not take him back.
		Lilly will not take Morgan back *even though* he has apologized three times.
Because	As a result	*Because* Julia is very friendly, she has numerous friends
		Julia has numerous friends *because* she is very friendly.
Since	As a result	*Since* the time change occurred, Walter has been feeling tired.
		Walter has been feeling tired *since* the time change.
When	Time specific	*When* my alarm goes off, I always hit snooze.
		I always hit snooze *when* my alarm goes off.

THINK *Write!*

Activity 17.6

Determine whether the following sentences are run-ons or comma splices. If they are run-ons, put an "RO" on the line preceding them. If they are comma splices, put a "CS." Then, correct the sentences using a subordinating word as directed. Remember when the subordinating word is the first word of the sentence, place a comma where the dependent clause ends.

1. _____ The basketball game went into triple overtime I got home after midnight.
   Use *Because* at the beginning of the sentence.

   _____

   _____

   Use *because* in the middle of the sentence. (HINT: You will have to rearrange the sentence to have it make sense.)

   _____

   _____

2. _____ Luis has a two-week vacation, he visits his grandparents in Costa Rica.
   Use *When* at the beginning of the sentence.

   _____

   _____

   Use *when* in the middle of the sentence. (Rearrange the sentence.)

   _____

   _____

3. _____ My car is filthy I do not have time to wash it.
   Use *Although* at the beginning of the sentence.

   _____

   _____

   Use *although* in the middle of the sentence. (Rearrange the sentence.)

   _____

   _____

THINK *Write!*

Activity 17.7

Correct the following run-on the four different ways as directed. Punctuate carefully as needed.

The runner sprained her ankle she was determined to finish the race.
   Correct using *but.*

1. _____

   _____

Correct using *however*.

2. _____
   _____

Use *Although* at the beginning of the sentence.

3. _____
   _____

Use *although* in the middle of the sentence.

4. _____
   _____

Correct the following comma splice the four different ways as directed. Punctuate carefully as needed.
The grizzly bear scared the campers, they fled the park.
   Use *so*.

5. _____
   _____

Use *therefore*.

6. _____
   _____

Use *Because* at the beginning of the sentence.

7. _____
   _____

Use *because* in the middle (you will need to arrange the sentence).

8. _____
   _____

Chapter 17 Review Exercise

Determine whether the following sentences are correct or not. If they are, put a "C" for correct on the line preceding them. If they are not, put an "RO" for run-on or a "CS" for comma splice.

Family Fun

1. _____ Every October my family and I go to the fair. 2. _____ We always have fun, there is so much to see and do. 3. _____ For example, I enjoy eating the food I am amazed at what can be fried. 4. _____ Fried butter, fried pickles, and fried turkey legs are my favorite. 5. _____ I cannot wait to see what the vendors will fry up this year, it could be either fried cotton candy or fried ice cream. 6. _____ While I enjoy the food, my husband enjoys looking at the new cars, he also likes to play the games on the Midway. 7. _____ Last year he won our daughter a gigantic teddy bear he had to shoot all three of the flying geese to win it. 8. _____ He kept playing the game until he won, for the amount of money he spent playing the game, he could have bought her a teddy bear at the store. 9. _____ Our kids enjoy having their dad win them prizes, riding the scary rides, and going into the house of mirrors. 10. _____ Although it is very expensive to go to the fair, we go every year because we always have a great time.

Commas

Commas, which are used to separate sentence elements, are one of the most misused punctuation marks. However, you must master this pesky punctuation mark; otherwise, you will sprinkle commas throughout your papers in the wrong places and leave them out where they need to be. After completing this chapter, you will have a thorough understanding of commas and will no longer have to fear these pesky punctuation marks.

Commas in a Series

Commas should be inserted with items in a series of three or more things.

- Words in a series: The locker room at the recreation center was hot, crowded, and smelly.

- Phrases in a series: Maria enjoys playing the piano, shopping for antiques, and volunteering at her daughter's school.

- Clauses in a series: Jasmine is in charge of ticket sells, Ricardo is handling publicity, and Tarik is supervising the volunteers.

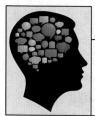 THINK *Write!*/TIP

Although clauses in a series may look similar to comma splices, they are not because a coordinating conjunction (and, but, or) connects the elements together into a correctly punctuated sentence. If, however, a comma and a conjunction are not in front of the last item in the series, then the sentence is a comma splice.

THINK *Write!*

Activity 18.1

Add commas in the following sentences that contain items in a series.

1. The movie was exciting action-packed and suspenseful.
2. Miranda enjoys reading dancing singing and drawing.
3. The apples in the garden the rice in the field and the grapes on the vines are ready to be picked.
4. The triplets all have high aspirations: Marco wants to be a pediatrician Miguel wants to be an engineer and Micaela wants to be a lawyer.
5. Jogging kick boxing and swimming are my stress busters.

Commas with Coordinating Conjunctions (FANBOYS)

Commas should be inserted when there is a complete sentence on BOTH sides of the FANBOYS.

, for   , and   , nor   , but   , or   , yet   , so

The comma goes in front of the conjunction and follows this pattern:

a complete sentence + comma and one of the FANBOYS + a complete sentence

✎ The baseball team won twelve games in a row, *so* they will definitely be in the playoffs.

✎ Jada went to the grocery store, *but* she left her list at home.

THINK *Write!*

Activity 18.2

Add one of the coordinating conjunctions (FANBOYS) to join the two independent clauses (, for , and , nor , but , or , yet , so).

1. I love to read, _____ one of my favorite authors is Maya Angelou.
2. James Patterson is another of my favorite authors, _____ I only like his books about the detective Alex Cross.
3. I also enjoy reading the books that my son reads, _____ I am currently reading *Hunger Games*.

4. My son and I go to the bookstore to get books, _____ we order them online.
5. My husband also likes to read, _____ he is cheap, _____ he only checks out books from the library, _____ that does not cost any money unless the books are turned in late.

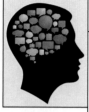

THINK *Write!* / TIP

Sometimes you think that whenever you see one of the FANBOYS, you are automatically supposed to insert a comma in front of it, but that is not the case. Rather, this is a compound verb. For more information on compound verbs, refer to Chapter 13: Subjects and Verbs. Commas should only be inserted if there are items in a series or a complete sentence on both sides of the FANBOYS.

THINK *Write!*

Activity 18.3

Underline the FANBOYS in the following sentences. If there is a complete sentence on BOTH sides of the FANBOYS, put a comma in front of the FANBOYS. Three sentences are correct.

1. Jessie likes to paint so most of her paycheck goes to buying art supplies.
2. Ryan enjoys fixing cars and racing them.
3. The country western star sang six songs and then she signed autographs.
4. The country western star sang six songs and then signed autographs.
5. Malik spends most of his time playing video games or downloading music on his I-pod.

Commas with Introductory Words, Phrases, and Clauses

Introductory Words

Commas should be inserted after introductory words when they are the first words of the sentence.

Common Introductory Words				
First,	Then,	Also,	Therefore,	For example,
Secondly,	Next,	In addition,	Consequently,	For instance,
Finally,	Lastly,	Furthermore,	However,	On the other hand,

THINK *Write!*

Activity 18.4

Add commas after the introductory words in the sentences below when they are the first word of the sentence. Four sentences are correct.

1. Steve admires Ramon because Ramon always has at least four girlfriends.
2. Therefore Steve decided to ask Ramon for advice on how to be a player.
3. Ramon laughed in Steve's face and refused to help him at first.
4. Then Ramon decided that he should share his skills with the less fortunate.
5. Ramon told Steve he needed to get rid of his geeky image.
6. For example he needed to put away his slide projector and get some longer pants.
7. Next he needed to talk to women about topics besides global warming and the demise of the Roman Empire.
8. Also Ramon told Steve he needed to sign up for some online dating services.
9. Steve took all of Ramon's advice.
10. Consequently Steve now has more dates than Ramon has.

Introductory Phrases

Commas should be used after introductory phrases.

✎ *In lieu of wedding gifts,* guests were asked to give donations to the couple's favorite charities.

✎ *To save money,* Michael brings his lunch to work three times a week.

✎ *Listening closely,* Christina was able to ease drop on several private conversations.

THINK *Write!*

Activity 18.5

Add commas after the introductory phrases.

1. On Tuesdays and Thursdays Rachel has three classes.
2. At 8 a.m. she has Spanish.
3. From 9:30 a.m. to 12:20 p.m. she has her English 1301/History 1301 Learning Community.
4. In the Learning Community she gets credit for two courses: English and history.
5. During the course the students write about what they study in the history course, work on projects, and go on field trips.

Introductory Clauses

Commas should be used after introductory clauses that begin with subordinating conjunctions.

✍ *Because my watch stopped working,* I was late to class.

✍ *If the Los Angeles Lakers win another championship,* I will become a fan.

✍ *Although Professor Martinez is very strict,* students enjoy being in her class.

Activity 18.6

Add commas after the introductory clauses.

1. If students have some free time in between classes they should begin reading the book.
2. While waiting for class to begin several students read the book.
3. After students read the book they will understand the movie better.
4. Although the book is over five hundred pages in length students should read the entire book.
5. When students finish the book they will want to read more books by the same author.

Activity 18.7

Add any necessary commas based on the three comma rules discussed so far:

✍ Commas with items in a series of three or more things
✍ Commas with FANBOYS when there is a complete sentence on both sides
✍ Commas after introductory words, phrases, and clauses.

On the blank line, write the comma rule. For the two sentences that do not need any commas, write "Correct" on the line.

1. When it rains Leonard loves to splash in puddles.

    _____

2. Leonard loves to splash in puddles when it rains.

    _____

3. The train was hot crowded and late.

    _____

4. Also the train was smelly.

    _____

5. The limo driver received a large tip so she was extremely happy.

    _____

6. In the middle of winter in Texas the temperature can be 75 degrees outside.

   _____

7. The printer is out of paper and ink.

   _____

8. The printer is out of paper and it is out of ink.

   _____

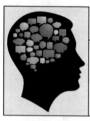

THINK *Write!*/TIP

As you write sentences, you will find that you use commas in a sentence for more than one reason. For example, you may write a sentence that contains an introductory word AND items in a series of three or more things. Therefore, you must analyze your sentences looking for multiple reasons for inserting commas instead of just one.

THINK *Write!*

Activity 18.8

Insert commas in the following sentences. Commas may be needed for more than one reason; therefore, you must review all of the comma rules so far. One sentence is correct.

1. Because I am shy I hate to speak in front of large crowds make small talk with strangers or participate in group discussions.
2. On the other hand Ricky loves to make presentations and he enjoys talking to strangers.
3. When Lulu is bored she gets on Facebook Twitter or My Space.
4. My favorite fruits are apples oranges strawberries and grapes; therefore I always have several of these in my refrigerator.
5. The little girl would not stop crying even though her mother promised to buy her some candy and a new doll.

Restrictive and Nonrestrictive Information

Commas with Which and That

Always use commas with the word *Which* to set off information because the information is extra or not needed. In other words, the information is nonrestrictive or not essential. Never use commas with the word *That* to set off information because the information is needed to make the sentence's meaning clear. In other words, the information is restrictive or essential.

✍ The English classes, *which were overloaded by three students,* were packed.

✍ The English classes *that were overloaded by three students* were packed.

While the two sentences above are almost identical, their meanings are completely different. The sentence that contains the *which* clause set off with commas means that ALL of the English classes were packed. Although it is interesting to know how many extra students were put into each English class, it is not necessary to know so, nor does it change the understanding of the sentence: *The English classes were packed.* Therefore, the word *which* is used, along with the commas.

On the other hand, the sentence that contains the word *that* not set off with commas means only some of the English classes were packed. To help make it clearer which classes were packed the *that* clause is added. This information is necessary or essential to know to help your readers understand the sentence or in this case to know that only the English classes that were overloaded were packed.

THINK *Write!*

Activity 18.9

Add any needed commas with *which* clauses. Do not add any commas with *that* clauses. Two sentences are correct.

1. The Van Gogh painting which is valued at $2.5 million is expected to go for nearly twice that at the upcoming auction.
2. The painting that is valued at $2.5 million is expected to go for nearly twice that amount at the upcoming auction.
3. Charming Charlie's which sells jewelry arranges its wares by color.
4. The store that sells jewelry that is arranged by color is very popular.

Who Clauses

Clauses that begin with *who* can be either nonrestrictive or restrictive; therefore, you must know when to use commas and when not to use commas.

Use commas when someone's specific name comes before the word *who*.

& Jason, who is very smart, tutors his classmates after class.

& Dr. Naim Lee, who served in the military for fifteen years, is very knowledgeable about the latest laser surgical procedures.

Do not use commas when a common noun comes before the word *who*.

& The student who has agreed to tutor his classmates after class is very smart.

& The doctor who served in the military for fifteen years is very knowledgeable about the latest surgical procedures.

EXCEPTION: If possessive pronouns, such as *my* or *our*, come before the common noun, then commas are needed.

& My oldest sister, who is a lawyer, volunteers at a free legal clinic on Thursday nights.

THINK *Write!*

Activity 18.10

In each pair below, one sentence needs commas and one does not. Add commas to the sentence that needs commas. Write "C" for correct by the correct sentence.

1. a. Olivia who specializes in Italian food is a very popular caterer.
    b. The woman who specializes in Italian food is a very popular caterer.
2. a. The singers who were auditioning for the female lead were asked to bring their resumes.
    b. Cori and Haven who were auditioning for the female lead were asked to bring their resumes.
3. a. Raymond who is a Chicago Bulls fan was so excited when he met Michael Jordan who is the world's best basketball player.
    b. The lucky Chicago Bulls fan was so excited when he met Michael Jordan.

Appositives

Appositives, which are nonrestrictive, provide additional and nonessential information about a noun or pronoun. Therefore, you set appositives off with commas.

- Lucy, the star of the *I Love Lucy* show, makes me laugh even before she says anything.
- My favorite group is Maze, led by Frankie Beverly.
- Eastfield College, one of the seven campuses of the DCCCD, is located in Mesquite, a suburban area near Dallas.

THINK *Write!*

Activity 18.11

Add commas as needed.

1. The trumpet oiled and shiny sounded brand new.
2. Valerie named after her grandmother just received her brown belt in karate.
3. Determined to win the boxer strode into the ring.

Lead-Ins for Lists

When the words *such as, especially, including,* and *like* are used, it usually means that some nonrestrictive information has been included; therefore, it is set off with a comma because it is not essential to the sentence. A comma comes before these words. However, no comma goes after them.

EXAMPLES

Students need to double check punctuation errors, *such as* the use of commas and semicolons.

I love all flavors of ice cream, *especially* chocolate, vanilla, and strawberry.

Everyone must get involved in stopping bullying, *including* students.

Apostrophes, like commas, are pesky punctuation marks.

THINK *Write!*

Activity 18.12

Add commas as needed.

1. The students made certain they had all of their supplies especially their calculators and notepads.
2. The tornado destroyed everything in the small town including the post office and the library.
3. The coach has a variety of motivational sayings such as "Only people who come in second place care that someone came in third," to encourage his players to always do their best.
4. The experienced hiker filled her backpack with useful things like fruit bars, bottled water, and a flare gun.

Use Commas with Interchangeable Adjectives

This rule is a little tricky because you have learned to put commas with items in a series of three or more things; however, this is the exception to that rule. A comma is used to separate two adjectives if the following conditions are met: the adjectives can be switched AND the word *and* can be inserted between them.

✆ The refreshing, cool water was appreciated after the six-mile hike.
The refreshing and cool water was appreciated after the six-mile hike.
The cool and refreshing water was appreciated after the six-mile hike.

✆ The light green suit is ugly.
The light and green suit is ugly. These cannot be switched
The green and light suit is ugly. Light must come before green.

THINK *Write!*

Activity 18.13

Add commas as needed.

1. The beautiful ornate quilt has been in Freddy's family for five generations.
2. The bright blue sunny sky was welcome after the dark gloomy night.
3. Little Julianna shrieked when her mother took away her ragged dirty doll.

Direct Quotations

Use Commas with Direct Quotations to Set off the Speaker

"I am so happy to have Ms. Rodriquez as my instructor," said Michael.

Michael said, "I am so happy to have Ms. Rodriquez as my instructor."

"I am so happy," Michael said, "to have Ms. Rodriquez as my instructor."

THINK *Write!*

Activity 18.14

Add commas as needed. One sentence is correct.

1. Murriel asked "Did you hear me on the radio last night?"
2. "No, I did not" replied Kenny.
3. "I did" said Kathryn "and you sounded great."
4. Murriel just beamed instead of replying.

Use Commas with Names When Speaking Directly to the Person

✎ Mary, where have you been?

✎ Where have you been, Mary?

Do not confuse speaking directly to the person with the person being the subject of the sentence or the direct object of the sentence.

Mary is very friendly and smart.

Mary is the subject of the sentence; no one is speaking directly to her.

We should ask **Mary** for help.

Mary is the direct object of the sentence; no one is speaking directly to her.

THINK *Write!*

Activity 18.15

Add commas as needed. Two sentences are correct.

1. I cannot believe Craig stood me up!
2. Richie do you know where Craig is?
3. Benjamin and Lenjamin are twins.
4. Are you and Lenjamin going to the party Benjamin?

Commas with Addresses and Dates

Addresses

Use commas with addresses to separate the items listed: the street address from the city and the city from the state or the country.

🐾 Geraldo lives at 2357 Elm St., Fort Worth, Texas 76116.

🐾 Mary used to live at 43 Seine Way, Paris, France, before moving back to the United States.

Dates

Use commas with dates to separate the items listed: the day of the week from the month and the day of the month from the year.

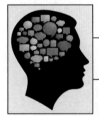

THINK *Write!* / TIP

> If a sentence that includes commas in the address or date continues on, insert a comma after the state or country or after the month or year.

THINK *Write!*

Activity 18.16

Add commas to separate the items in addresses and dates as needed. One sentence is correct.

1. Bon Jovi is scheduled to perform at the American Airlines Center on Saturday July 18.
2. I asked my doctor to call in my prescription to the Walgreens that is located at 5501 Main St. Ft. Lauderdale Florida.
3. Mark and Jennifer plan to renew their vows on a Sunday in September.
4. President John F. Kennedy was assassinated on November 11 1963 in Dallas Texas.

Chapter 18 Review Exercise

Add twenty-five commas using all of the comma rules discussed in this chapter.

The Annoying Fire Drill

Before the 9:30 a.m. classes started on Thursday my college had a fire drill. My fellow students the professors the administrators the professional support staff and I had to exit the buildings. I was annoyed because I had to stand outside carrying all of the items I had brought to school such as my back pack my guitar and my art portfolio. The fire marshal was happy that everyone exited the buildings quickly so we did not have to stand outside for a long time. If people take their time leaving the buildings we have to stand outside for thirty minutes or longer. I know the drills are important but I hate standing outside when I could be doing something else. As we stand outside, we have to listen to the people who are wearing bright yellow jackets. Mary who is wearing a bright yellow jacket is in charge of evacuating the C building. Mary shouted "Move away from the building now or I will have you arrested." A rebellious outspoken student refused to move away from the building. The student angry about standing outside was arrested for refusing to follow orders. As the student was being led away in handcuffs he looked at Mary and said "Mary you are taking this drill a little too seriously." The next drill is scheduled for Tuesday February 25. I plan to be absent that day. After a fire drill Starbucks which is my favorite place to study is always crowded because students go there instead of standing outside.

Chapter 19

Commonly Confused Words

Sometimes words sound the same but are spelled differently. It is extremely important that you choose the correct word in order to convey the correct meaning to the reader. In this chapter, you are asked to think about the spelling and meaning of words. Below are some words that you may confuse with other words that have different meanings.

Word 1	Meaning	Word 2	Meaning	Example Sentences
A	Article used before words that begin with a consonant sound	An	Article used before words that begin with a vowel sound	1. Sinbad is *a* hilarious comedian. 2. Liza needs *an* X-ray taken of her foot.
Accept	To agree to receive or do	Except	Not including	1. I *accept* your apology. 2. I want all the clothes *except* the red shirt.
Advice	Recommendations about what to do	Advise	To recommend something	1. Helen gives good *advice*. 2. She always *advises* everyone to make good choices.
Affect	To change or make a difference to	Effect	A result; to bring about a result	1. The neighborhood was *affected* by the hurricane. 2. The special *effects* were poor.

(continued)

Word 1	Meaning	Word 2	Meaning	Example Sentences
Aisle	A passage between rows of seats	Isle	An island	1. Melanie walked down the *aisle* of the plane. 2. The Caribbean *isle* is lovely.
All together	All in one place, all at once	Altogether	Completely; on the whole	1. The whole family was *all together* in Aspen. 2. *Altogether*, I do not like it.
Along	Moving or extending horizontally on	A long	Referring to something of great length	1. Maribel went *along* with Jose. 2. It is *a long* road.
Aloud	Out loud	Allowed	Permitted	1. Penelope accidently said what she was thinking *out loud*. 2. The dog is *allowed* on the couch.
Altar	A sacred table in a church or religious center	Alter	To change	1. Harold worshipped at the *altar*. 2. Daisy *altered* her hair cut.
Among	Used when discussing three or more things/people	Between	Used when discussing only two things/people	1. Evelyn was chosen from *among* all the students to represent the school at the state speech contest. 2. The book fell *between* the chair and the end table.
Amoral	Not concerned with right or wrong	Immoral	Not following accepted moral standards	1. Charles Manson is an *amoral* person. 2. *Immoral* people are often shunned by society.
Assent	Agreement, approval	Ascent	The action of rising or climbing up	1. Kanella *assented* to let the twins go to the party. 2. The *ascent* to the top of the mountain was difficult.
Bare	Naked; to uncover	Bear	To carry; to put up with	1. Jimmy *bared* his chest. 2. Angelica had to *bear* the weight of the guilt because she betrayed Andre.
Bazaar	A Middle Eastern market	Bizarre	Strange	1. Jane shopped at the Moroccan *bazaar*. 2. Bill is such a *bizarre* fellow.
Born	Having started life	Borne	Carried	1. Cynthia was *born* in May. 2. The weight of the travel pack was *borne* by Jorge.

Word 1	Meaning	Word 2	Meaning	Example Sentences
Bough	A branch of a tree	Bow	To bend the head; the front of a ship	1. The tree *bough* broke in the storm. 2. The people *bowed* to the king and queen.
Brake	A device for stopping a vehicle; to stop a vehicle	Break	To separate into pieces; a pause	1. Owen pressed the *brake* pedal to stop the car. 2. It hurts to *break* one's arm. 3. Spring *break* is fun.
Breath	Noun form referring to the intake of air	Breathe	Verb form referring to the action of inhaling air	1. Eduardo could not catch his *breath*. 2. The air was smoggy, and it was hard to *breathe*.
Breach	To break through, or break a rule; a gap	Breech	The back part of a gun barrel	1. An iceberg *breached* the *Titanic's* hull. 2. The gun *breech* cracked and broke when it hit the ground.
Buy	Purchase	By	Beside; through	1. I want to *buy* that new video game. 2. Pratik drove *by* the college.
Canvas	A type of strong cloth	Canvass	To seek people's votes, opinions; to find out information from others	1. The sail was made of *canvas*. 2. Devon *canvassed* the neighborhood.
Censure	To criticize strongly	Censor	To ban parts of a book or film; a person who does this	1. The FCC *censured* the radio station for obscene language and then fined them thousands of dollars. 2. The government *censored* the newspaper because of libelous statements.
Cereal	A grass producing an edible grain; a breakfast food made from grains	Serial	Happening in a series	1. Tommy eats *cereal* for breakfast. 2. Smallville, a television *serial*, was my favorite show.
Chord	A group of musical notes	Cord	A length of string; a cord-like body part	1. Adam played the *chord* on his guitar. 2. The *cord* of rope was very thick.

(continued)

Word 1	Meaning	Word 2	Meaning	Example Sentences
Coarse	Rough	Course	A direction; a school subject; part of a meal	1. The *coarse* material scratched Grant's face. 2. The developmental writing *course* was enlightening.
Complement	To add to so as to improve; an addition that improves something	Compliment	To praise or express approval; an admiring remark	1. The new tutoring center *complemented* the college's mission of excellence in teaching and learning. 2. Ricky *complimented* Lucy on her new haircut.
Council	A group of people who manage or advise	Counsel	Advice; to advise	1. The *council* passed the bill. 2. Harry *counseled* Urica about which college to attend.
Cue	A signal for action; a wooden rod	Queue	A line of people or vehicles	1. The lightning crash was Maria's *cue* to go on stage. 2. The movie theatre *queue* seemed a mile long.
Currant	A dried grape	Current	Happening now; a flow of water, air, or electricity	1. Lyle does not like *currants*. 2. The river *current* is fast in this area.
Defuse	To make a situation less tense	Diffuse	To spread over a wide area	1. Elias *defused* the argument between Joe and Kasey. 2. The smell of the perfume *diffused* throughout the room.
Desert	A waterless, empty area; to abandon someone	Dessert	The sweet course of a meal	1. The *desert* can be a dangerous place. 2. Wendy's favorite *dessert* is pineapple upside down cake.
Discreet	Careful not to attract attention	Discrete	Separate and distinct	1. Oliver tried to sneak into work late, but he was not *discreet* enough. 2. The men's dressing room and the women's dressing room must be *discrete* in order to preserve privacy.
Disinterested	Impartial	Uninterested	Not interested	1. Roberto was *disinterested* in the fact that Pablo and Karen had gotten back together. 2. Many people are *uninterested* in politics today.

Word 1	Meaning	Word 2	Meaning	Example Sentences
Dual	Having two parts	Duel	A fight or contest between two people	1. The developmental writing class has a *dual* exit exam. 2. Alexander Hamilton was killed in a *duel* with Aaron Burr.
Elicit	To draw out a reply or reaction	Illicit	Not allowed by law or rules	1. The reporter attempted to *elicit* a response from the politician. 2. Upton's *illicit* behavior resulted in suspension from the college.
Ensure	To make certain that something will happen	Insure	To provide compensation if a person dies or property is damaged	1. Isabelle studied to *ensure* a high grade in her history class. 2. Quentin *insured* his house against tornado damage.
Envelop	To cover or surround	Envelope	A paper container for a letter	1. Rachel was *enveloped* in a soft blanket. 2. I mailed my bills in brown *envelopes*.
Farther	Use for physical distance	Further	Use for figurative distance	1. Narcedalia walked *farther* down the street than last week. 2. The psychology class will *further* one's understanding of Sigmund Freud's theories.
Feel	Touch; have emotion	Fill	To make full	1. I do not *feel* well. 2. I *filled* my belly with too much food.
Flaunt	To display ostentatiously	Flout	To disregard a rule	1. Willis *flaunted* his new car. 2. Tara *flouted* the rules by lighting a cigarette in the non-smoking section of the restaurant.
Flounder	To move clumsily; to have difficulty doing something	Founder	To fail; one who establishes something; to sink	1. Raul *floundered* in the shallow water of the pool. 2. The internet business *foundered* when the economy went into a recession.
Foreword	An introduction to a book	Forward	Onward, ahead	1. Illiana read the textbook's *foreword*. 2. Opal moved *forward* with the project.

(continued)

Word 1	Meaning	Word 2	Meaning	Example Sentences
Good	Adjective—can only describe nouns and pronouns	Well	Adverb—can only describe actions, adjectives, or other adverbs	1. Morgan did a *good* job on her assignment. 2. Ramon also did *well*.
Himself	Reflexive/intensive form of he	Hisself	Not a word—do not use	1. Jesse got *himself* suspended when he smoked a cigarette in the bathroom.
Imply	To suggest indirectly	Infer	To draw a conclusion	1. You do not need to stay "I think" in a thesis statement; it is *implied*. 2. From the white paint transfer marks on my bumper, I can *infer* someone hit me and drove off afterward.
Its	Possessive form of it	It's	Contraction of it is or it has	1. The dog chases *its* tail. 2. *It's* going to rain tomorrow.
Loath	Reluctant, unwilling	Loathe	To hate	1. I am *loath* to go to work today. 2. Jessica *loathes* tomatoes.
Loose	To unfasten; to set free	Lose	To be deprived of; to be unable to find	1. Since Lester lost weight, his pants are *loose*. 2. Kevin always *loses* his keys.
Past	Time frame that already happened; beyond	Passed	Went by	1. The argument is in the *past*. 2. I walked *past* the church for the first time yesterday. 3. Gregory *passed* all his classes!
Pole	A long, slender piece of wood	Poll	Voting in an election	1. The light *pole* was blown over in the wind. 2. The *poll* showed Ben would win the school election.
Pour	To flow or cause to flow	Pore	A tiny opening; to study something closely	1. Nancy *poured* water into a glass. 2. Alan *pored* over his homework.
Principal	Most important; the head of a school	Principle	A fundamental rule or belief	1. The *principal* is my pal. 2. The *principles* of writing can be mastered with practice.
Sight	The ability to see	Site	A location	1. Carson's *sight* was perfect after his LASIK surgery. 2. The building *site* was on the lakeshore.

Word 1	Meaning	Word 2	Meaning	Example Sentences
Stationary	Not moving	Stationery	Writing materials	1. The *stationary* bike is an excellent exercise tool. 2. Felicia uses her personal *stationery* to answer correspondence.
Then	Shows time; cause and effect	Than	Makes a comparison	1. *Then*, Ellenore went to the movies with Neil. 2. She likes Neil better *than* her old boyfriend.
Tortuous	Full of twists; complex	Torturous	Full of pain or suffering	1. The maze was *tortuous*. 2. Roger's headache was *torturous*.
Use	To put into service	Used to	Something done previously	1. On Sundays, we *use* the good dishes. 2. Cathy *used to* live in New York.
Wreath	A ring-shaped arrangement of flowers, etc.	Wreathe	To surround or encircle	1. The holiday *wreath* on the Summers' door is lovely. 2. The religious altar was *wreathed* with candles.
Your	Possessive form of you	You're	Contraction of you are or you were	1. Is this *your* backpack? 2. *You're* going to get in trouble.

Below are some of the commonly confused words that have three or more confused forms of words.

Word	Meaning
Quiet	Hushed
Quit	Stop
Quite	Very

EXAMPLE SENTENCES

The library is a *quiet* place.

Xander *quit* his job at the warehouse.

The weather is *quite* lovely today.

Word	Meaning
Their	A pronoun referring to themselves or them
There	In or at that place
They're	Contraction of they are

EXAMPLE SENTENCES

The Shepherds are a very sweet family, and *their* house is always clean.

There is one room in the house that is mess though: the guest room.

They're in the process of remodeling it.

Word	Meaning
Themselves	Reflexive/intensive pronoun form of they
Themselves	Not a word
Theirself	Not a word
Theirselves	Not a word

EXAMPLE SENTENCES

The students wondered to *themselves* if they had made good grades on their tests.

Word	Meaning
Through	In at one end and out at the other
Thorough	Extremely attentive to accuracy and detail
Threw	The past tense of throw; to propel an object

EXAMPLE SENTENCES

The car sped *through* the tunnel.

The police did a *thorough* investigation of the stolen museum paintings.

Rhonda accidentally *threw* the baseball through the window while playing catch.

Word	Meaning
To	To indicate direction
Too	Also or very
Two	The number 2

EXAMPLE SENTENCES

Paul is going *to* Palm Beach for spring break.

Allison is taking a ballet class, and Miriam wants to take one *too*.

There are *two* windows on the side of the house that need to be cleaned.

Word	Meaning
Weather	Outdoor atmosphere including temperature, rain, sun, etc.
Whether	Two possibilities
Rather	Prefer to, instead

EXAMPLE SENTENCES

The *weather* can quickly become dangerous in Oklahoma during spring.

I love cats *whether* they are long haired or short haired.

I would *rather* have a short haired cat though.

Word	Meaning
Where	Refers to place
Were	Past tense form of be in third person plural
Wear	To put on
Ware	Goods
We're	Contraction of we are or we were

EXAMPLE SENTENCES

Where are the restrooms?

They *were* down the hall, but renovations caused them to be moved.

Cee Lo Green always seems to *wear* red clothes.

Street vendors sell their *wares* in parks in New York City.

We're going to buy knock off Prada bags from them.

THINK  *Write!*

Activity 19.1

Examine each sentence to determine if the underlined confused words are correct. If the word is not correct, cross out the word and write the correct spelling of it above the word.

1. <u>Accept</u> for Susan, I will not <u>except</u> any late work.
2. <u>We're</u> in the world <u>where</u> you? We <u>wear</u> looking all over for you.
3. <u>Weather</u> the <u>whether</u> is bad or not, <u>there</u> going over <u>their too</u> mow the lawn today.
4. The <u>principal</u> idea is to please the <u>principle</u> and not make him have to repeat <u>hisself</u>.
5. After the young mother scolded her children, they <u>where</u> very <u>quite</u>.
6. He is <u>a</u> honorable man, so I was <u>quiet</u> shocked when he was arrested for an <u>elicit</u> scheme.
7. In high school, Rhonda took <u>too duel</u> credit courses.

8. LaShawn saw the most <u>bizarre</u> thing as she waited to <u>feel</u> her Accord with gas.
9. Michelle is not <u>aloud</u> to have <u>desert</u> unless she eats all of her dinner.
10. Every morning Richard jogs three miles and <u>than</u> he eats a bowl of <u>serial</u>.

THINK *Write!*

Activity 19.2

Underline the correct confused word.

1. The proud father walked the bride down the (aisle, isle) and up to the (altar, alter).
2. Richenda's (stationary, stationery) has her initials on it.
3. Amy and Regina (loath, loathe) (their, there, they're) math class.
4. When we (wear, we're, were) looking for (your, you're) house, we drove right (passed, past) it.
5. Sheila did a (good, well) job on her book report; in fact, she did so (good, well) Professor Jackson wants to (use, used to) it as a model paper for the other students.
6. (Weather, Whether) or not Jessie apologizes, Gina will not take him back.
7. Tina would (weather, whether, rather) be on the beach (than, then) anywhere else.
8. Miguel (use, used to) live in Costa Rica before moving to the United States.
9. "(Its, It's) (to, too, two) cold in here!" whined Rebecca. "I cannot take a test under these (tortuous, torturous) conditions."
10. (Their, There, They're) the cutest couple. They spend all of (their, there, they're) time together. (Their, There, They're) is never a moment when (their, there, they're) around.

THINK *Write!*

Activity 19.3

On notebook paper, write the definitions for the following commonly confused words. Then, write a sentence using each word correctly.

1. Accept/except
2. Imply/infer
3. Principle/principal
4. Farther/ further
5. Affect/effect

Chapter 19 Review Exercise

Circle the incorrectly used commonly confused words. Then, write the correct words above. There are fifteen commonly confused words errors.

Mari's Mission: The Hunt for Scholarship Money

After being excepted into the college of her dreams, Mari decided not too attend summer school. Instead, she wanted to use the time to relax, to prepare her mind for the upcoming fall semester, and to apply for scholarships. She asked her principle for a letter of reference so that she could include it with her materials as she applied for more scholarship money. Since Mari was planning to major in theater, it would be important for her to earn as much money as she could in order to farther her education. Mari's parents were concerned because they did not know weather or not she would get the scholarship money in time; however, they knew that if their wear any funds to be found, Mari would know were to look. After two weeks past, Mari decided to go to the public library to research the scholarships that where available. She found several theater scholarships that offered quiet a lot of monetary assistance. She choose to that if awarded would pay for both her tuition and her room and board. She contacted her academic advisor for advise on applying for the scholarships. After a long six-week waiting period, Mari was granted both scholarships. As a result, Mari was able too relax for the rest of the summer and prepare for her new adventures in college.

Verb and Tense Shifts

Verb Tense

In English, tenses are used to show time. The tense tells the reader when something is occurring. There are several verb tenses in the English language. The charts below represent the verb tenses using the verb *walk*.

SIMPLE PRESENT TENSE

Person	Singular	Plural
First Person	I walk	We walk
Second Person	You walk	You walk
Third Person	He/she/it walks	They walk

PRESENT PROGRESSIVE TENSE

Person	Singular	Plural
First Person	I am walking	We are walking
Second Person	You are walking	You are walking
Third Person	He/she/it is walking	They are walking

PRESENT PERFECT TENSE

Person	Singular	Plural
First Person	I have walked	We have walked
Second Person	You have walked	You have walked
Third Person	He/she/it has walked	They have walked

SIMPLE PAST TENSE

Person	Singular	Plural
First Person	I walked	We walked
Second Person	You walked	You walked
Third Person	He/she/it walked	They walked

PAST PROGRESSIVE TENSE

Person	Singular	Plural
First Person	I was walking	We were walking
Second Person	You were walking	You were walking
Third Person	He/she/it was walking	They were walking

PAST PERFECT TENSE

Person	Singular	Plural
First Person	I had walked	We had walked
Second Person	You had walked	You had walked
Third Person	He/she/it had walked	They had walked

SIMPLE FUTURE TENSE

Person	Singular	Plural
First Person	I will walk	We will walk
Second Person	You will walk	You will walk
Third Person	He/she/it will walk	They will walk

FUTURE PROGRESSIVE TENSE

Person	Singular	Plural
First Person	I will be walking	We will be walking
Second Person	You will be walking	You will be walking
Third Person	He/she/it will be walking	They will be walking

FUTURE PERFECT TENSE

Person	Singular	Plural
First Person	I will have walked	We will have walked
Second Person	You will have walked	You will have walked
Third Person	He/she/it will have walked	They will have walked

Irregular Verbs

Walk is considered a regular verb. It does not do anything irregular when it becomes past tense. With play, "-ed" is added. However, there are many irregular verbs in the English language that do not follow the standard tense rules. Generally speaking, the irregularities occur in simple past tense and all of the perfect tenses. Look below for a chart of common irregular verbs.

Base Form of Verb	Simple Past	Perfect (Participle)
Be	Was/were	Has/have/had been
Become	Became	Has/have/had become
Begin	Began	Has/have/had begun
Blow	Blew	Has/have/had blown
Break	Broke	Has/have/had broken
Bring	Brought	Has/have/had brought
Buy	Bought	Has/have/had bought
Catch	Caught	Has/have/had caught
Choose	Chose	Has/have/had chosen
Come	Came	Has/have/had come
Do	Did	Has/have/had done
Draw	Drew	Has/have/had drawn
Drink	Drank	Has/have/had drunk
Drive	Drove	Has/have/had driven
Eat	Ate	Has/have/had eaten
Fall	Fell	Has/have/had fallen
Feel	Felt	Has/have/had felt
Fight	Fought	Has/have/had fought
Find	Found	Has/have/had found
Fly	Flew	Has/have/had flown
Freeze	Froze	Has/have/had frozen
Get	Got	Has/have/had gotten
Give	Gave	Has/have/had given

(continued)

Base Form of Verb	Simple Past	Perfect (Participle)
Go	Went	Has/have/had gone
Grow	Grew	Has/have/had grown
Have	Had	Has/have/had had
Hear	Heard	Has/have/had heard
Hide	Hid	Has/have/had hidden
Hold	Held	Has/have/had held
Hurt	Hurt	Has/have/had hurt
Keep	Kept	Has/have/had kept
Lay	Laid	Has/have/had laid
Lead	Led	Has/have/had led
Leave	Left	Has/have/had left
Lend	Lent	Has/have/had lent
Lie	Lay	Has/have/had lain
Lose	Lost	Has/have/had lost
Put	Put	Has/have/had put
Ride	Rode	Has/have/had ridden
Rise	Rose	Has/have/had risen
Run	Ran	Has/have/had run
See	Saw	Has/have/had seen
Sing	Sang	Has/have/had sung
Sit	Sat	Has/have/had sat
Speak	Spoke	Has/have/had spoken
Swim	Swam	Has/have/had swum
Take	Took	Has/have/had taken
Tear	Tore	Has/have/had torn
Throw	Threw	Has/have/had thrown
Write	Wrote	Has/have/had written

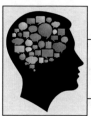

THINK *Write!* TIP

Be is one of the most irregular verbs in the English language. It is irregular in almost every verb tense. Be careful when working with *be!* The many forms of be include *am, is, are, was, were, been, being,* and more.

Unnecessary Tense Shifts

One common mistake that you may make is shifting from one verb tense to another when it is unnecessary. Usually this is from present tense to past tense or from past tense to present tense. One writing mode that is particularly susceptible to this error is the narrative. Although sometimes tense shifts are necessary, you need to be careful when using them; tense shifts should only occur when needed.

THINK *Write!*

Activity 20.1

Make corrections to tense shifts in the following sentences. If the sentence starts in present tense, it should remain in present. If it starts in past tense, keep it in the past.

1. Kerry often spends time out in his office drawing elaborate airplane designs; later in the afternoons, he discussed them with his friend, Rick.

2. Demetrius went to the fair last Saturday, and he spends all day riding the ship and the roller coaster.

3. The notebook was found over by the bus stop, so some of the students turn it in to the lost and found.

4. The crystal staircase is one of the largest in the world, but most people did not know about it.

5. Cell phones have become serious distractions in the classroom, and many professors did not allow them out during class anymore.

THINK *Write!*

Activity 20.2

Write a paragraph about the day you graduated from high school and/or received your GED. Because this already happened, keep it in past tense.

_____

_____

_____

_____

_____

_____

THINK *Write!*

Activity 20.3

Write a paragraph about your morning routine. Because it is something that happens every day, you should use present tense for this paragraph.

_____

_____

_____

_____

_____

_____

_____

_____

_____

_____

Active and Passive Voice

Another error that often occurs in writing is using passive voice instead of active voice.

Active Voice

Active voice occurs when the subject of the verb completes the action of the verb.

EXAMPLE

Suzanne lost the library book.

Passive Voice

Passive voice occurs when the subject of the verb is no longer completing the action of the verb but rather is being acted upon.

EXAMPLE

The library book was lost by Suzanne.

Although passive voice is occasionally necessary, active voice is preferred because it reads more smoothly and sounds less clunky. Using passive voice creates the need for a helping verb ("was" in the example) and almost always requires the word *by* in front of the subject. Using passive voice reverses the order of the subject and verb as well, which can sometimes really gum up a sentence for a reader. This is the reason it is generally considered better to use active voice for most writing, constructing the majority of your sentences in the subject-verb-object pattern.

THINK *Write!*

Activity 20.4

Turn the passive voice sentences below into active voice sentences.

1. The computer was turned on by Logan.

    _____

2. The curtain was closed by Oliver.

    _____

3. The color guard flag was tossed by Blakely.

    _____

4. The goal was scored by Rylin.

    _____

5. The dance was performed by Scarlett.

    _____

Chapter 20 Review Exercise

Read through the paragraph below and make ten corrections to tense shifts.

Holiday Cheer

The holidays are such a wonderful time of year. My three favorite holiday activities are decorating for Halloween, decorating for Christmas, and going on my family's annual Christmas light tour. Decorating for Halloween was something I look forward to all year. I have four boxes full of Halloween decorations. I strung lights on the porch and put spider webs on the bushes. Close to Halloween my husband and I carve jack-o-lanterns to put on the porch, and we always put pumpkin candles in them to make our porch smell delicious when the trick-or-treaters came. I also have indoor decorations, like pumpkins, ghosts, witches, and black cats. Another holiday activity I enjoy is decorating for Christmas. My husband and I loved Christmas lights, and we put them all over our house. I climb on the roof and line the gutters with colored lights while my husband wrapped red and white lights around our porch column to make a candy cane. Inside, we hung garland and lights. Midway through December we get our live Christmas tree and decorated it with all our old ornaments. Last year we had so many, we could not hang them all on the tree. Lastly, I enjoy taking our family's annual Christmas light tour. First, we go out to dinner at an upscale restaurant or a favorite place we enjoy eating at. Afterward, we piled in the car and drive around town looking at people's decorations. One of the best neighborhoods to look at for lights is in Mesquite, Texas, just off I-30. Almost all of the houses are decorated, and children sold hot chocolate on the corners. At one house, they have carolers on Fridays and Saturdays to serenade the viewers with Christmas songs. I absolutely loved the holidays, and three of my favorite holiday activities are decorating for Halloween and Christmas and going on my family's Christmas light tour.

Pronouns and Pronoun–Antecedent Agreement

Pronouns

Pronouns are words that replace a noun.

Subjective Case

Subjective case pronouns can be used as the subject of a sentence.

Person	Singular	Plural
First	I	We
Second	You	You
Third	He/she/it	They

EXAMPLES

I always remember to brush my teeth before bed.

We cannot wait to take our spring break trip to the Bahamas.

They are brand new shoes.

Objective Case

Objective case pronouns can be used as the object of a sentence.

Person	Singular	Plural
First	Me	Us
Second	You	You
Third	Him/her/it	Them

EXAMPLES

The key ring belongs to *her*.

The book was written for *them*.

He brought the donuts for *us*.

Possessive Case

Possessive case pronouns show ownership.

Person	Singular	Plural
First	My/mine	Our/ours
Second	Your/yours	Your/yours
Third	His/her/hers/its	Their/theirs

EXAMPLES

"Smells Like Teen Spirit" is *his* favorite song.

Her closet is very disorganized.

Your essay was very well written.

That carport is *theirs*.

Reflexive and Intensive Case

Reflexive pronouns show action that was performed by someone to himself/herself. Intensive pronouns are used for emphasis and are identical to reflexive pronouns.

Person	Singular	Plural
First	Myself	Ourselves
Second	Yourself	Yourselves
Third	Himself/herself/itself	Themselves

REFLEXIVE EXAMPLES

Julia looked *herself* over in the mirror before leaving for work.

Christina and Samantha bought *themselves* silly hats to wear for the costume party.

INTENSIVE EXAMPLES

The superintendent *herself* delivered the graduation speech.

The house *itself* is quite beautiful.

Who vs. Whom

Who and *whom* create pronoun case problems. The problem occurs because *who* is subjective while *whom* is objective. Below is a trick to know when to use *who* and when to use *whom*.

- If the sentence can be rephrased to use one of the objective pronouns, like *him/her/them*, then use *whom*. If the sentence can be rearranged to use one of the subjective pronouns, like *he/she/it/they*, then choose *who*.

- For example, the novel title *For Whom the Bell Tolls* can be rearranged to say "the bell tolls for him." Therefore, *whom* is required.

- On the other hand, the book title *The Girl Who Played with Fire* can be rearranged to say "she played with fire." Therefore, *who* is needed this time.

- It works with questions as well. If the question can be answered with an objective pronoun, use *whom*. If the question is answered with a subjective pronoun, use *who*.
  - Whom is the gift for? The gift is for him.
  - Who is in the office? He is in the office.

THINK *Write!*

Activity 21.1

Choose who or whom to correct the sentences below.

1. (Who/Whom) is going to bring the cake?
2. (Who/Whom) will the benefit concert proceeds go to?
3. To (who/whom) should I label this package?
4. The man (who/whom) has a handlebar mustache is the star of a Wild West show.
5. David, (who/whom) I know, was going to be named to city council before the scandal occurred.

Pronoun–Antecedent Agreement

Pronoun–antecedent agreement is an important rule to memorize for polished writing. It is similar to subject–verb agreement, and some of the same rules can be applied.

Antecedent

The antecedent is the word the pronoun replaces.

The Rule of Pronoun–Antecedent Agreement

Pronouns and their antecedents must agree in number and gender. Therefore, if the antecedent is plural, the pronoun must be plural, and if the antecedent is feminine, for example, the pronoun must be feminine, as well.

EXAMPLES

The **flag** was tossed high in the air, but *it* got caught by the wind and was carried off.

> The "flag" is the antecedent; it is singular and has no gender, so "it" is used

Daniela and Juan planned a fabulous trip to the beach because *their* vacation times coincided this year.

> "Daniela" and "Juan" are the antecedent; they are plural, so "their" is used

Stephen was born in Ohio, but *he* grew up in the Midwest.

> "Stephen" is the antecedent; he is singular and masculine, so "he" is used.

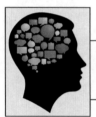 THINK *Write!* / TIP

> Sometimes making corrections to pronoun–antecedent agreement can cause errors in subject–verb agreement. When this occurs, be sure to make corrections to subjects and verbs, as well.

THINK *Write!*

Activity 21.2

Correct errors to pronoun–antecedent agreement in the sentences below. Be aware that changes may need to be made to the verbs to make sure they agree, as well.

1. Ramen noodles are delicious, and it is my favorite lunch.

2. The horse galloped happily across the fields, clearly invigorated after having their saddle removed.

3. Catalita stared up at the gargoyles; its grotesque faces gave her an uneasy feeling.

4. Courtney decided to go shopping after work because they got off work early.

5. The children went out to the playground to swing on the tire swing, but Karolina could not go because she forgot its coat.

Problems with Pronouns and Pronoun–Antecedent Agreement

One problem with pronoun–antecedent agreement occurs when the gender of a singular antecedent is not known. For example, "a student" as an antecedent has no clear gender. However, it is singular. Therefore, it is necessary to choose *he/she, his/her,* or *him/her* as the pronoun to replace it.

EXAMPLES

A student has brought *his/her* essay to the office for grading.

A child played by *himself/herself* with an imaginary friend.

The professor made the test from *his/her* memory.

Because all of the examples have singular antecedents but unknown genders, the pronouns for both genders must be used. If they are plural, it makes it easier; just use *they, them,* or *their.*

THINK

Activity 21.3

Correct errors to pronoun–antecedent agreement with unknown gender in singular and plural below.

1. The lawyer is never in their office when people need to speak with them.

2. The child counted to one hundred after learning their numbers.

3. The teachers will be able to finish his/her grading faster if classes are cancelled for the day.

4. The student engineers will have his/her designs judged by professionals.

5. All the children wanted to wear different costumes to his/her school Halloween party.

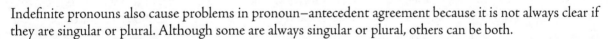

Indefinite pronouns also cause problems in pronoun–antecedent agreement because it is not always clear if they are singular or plural. Although some are always singular or plural, others can be both.

These four indefinite pronouns are always plural. Therefore, they will always match to a plural antecedent or pronoun and take a plural verb.

Both	Few	Many	Several

EXAMPLES

Both of the police officers took **their** lunch in the squad car.

Several of the students brought **their** favorite books to class to share.

These sixteen indefinite pronouns are always singular. Therefore, they will always match to a singular antecedent or pronoun and take a singular verb.

Everyone	Anyone	Someone	No one
Everybody	Anybody	Somebody	Nobody
Everything	Anything	Something	Nothing
Each	Either	Neither	One

EXAMPLES

Everyone in the room can bring **his/her** laptop tomorrow.

One of the children forgot **his/her** lunch.

These five indefinite pronouns can be singular or plural. You have to check the context of the sentence to make sure you are using them correctly.

All	Any	Most	None	Some

EXAMPLES

All of the *chairs* had **their** seats broken.

> In this sentence, it is clear that "all" is plural because of "chairs," so use "their" instead of "its."

Some of the *cake* was eaten, and later **it** was all gone.

> In this sentence, "some" is singular because of "cake," so use "it" instead of "they."

THINK *Write!*

Activity 21.4

Make corrections to pronoun–antecedent errors involving indefinite pronouns in the sentences below. Remember that changes to the verbs may need to be made, as well. Each sentence has two errors.

1. Neither of the students had their homework prepared when they arrived in class this morning.

2. All of the girls wore brand new dresses and had ribbons in her hair and new shoes on her feet.

3. Any person found trespassing on the Jones Street property will be arrested on sight; they will be charged with trespassing, and the state will fine them.

4. Most of the cookies Sharon made have been eaten; it was so delicious that the staff could not help eating it all up.

5. Several of the parents came to school early to pick up his/her children after testing was over; he/she wanted to take the children out to lunch as a reward.

Chapter 21 Review Exercise

Make ten corrections to pronoun–antecedent agreement errors in the paragraph below.

Yes to Sex Ed Classes

Sex education should be a required course in public schools in the United States for many reasons. First, some parents do not talk to his/her children about sex; in fact, neither parent may be comfortable talking to their child about this matter. These children then have to figure it out for himself/herself. It is the school's responsibility to teach these students about his/her bodies and sex. Furthermore, these classes could help decrease teen pregnancy. If teens took sex education classes, he/she could learn more about contraception and abstinence. Knowledge is powerful, and teens may make better decisions about his/her lives. Finally, sex education classes will allow students to learn about sexually transmitted diseases. AIDS and HIV are dangerous diseases; it could potentially kill someone who contracted it, and students need to know this. Other STDs that could affect him/her are chlamydia, gonorrhea, and HPV. If teens were aware of the consequences of sex, it would help him/her make better decisions. All public schools should require sex education classes.

Apostrophes

Apostrophes, like commas, sometimes get sprinkled in your writing in places where they are not supposed to be. Therefore, you must look out for apostrophes and know when to use them and when not to use them. Basically, apostrophes are used two ways: to form contractions and to show ownership.

Apostrophes in Contractions

A contraction is a word that is formed by joining two words into one with an apostrophe. The apostrophe takes the place of the missing letter or letters.

Chart of Commonly Used Contractions	
I am	I'm
Do not	Don't
Can not	Can't
Could not	Couldn't
It is, it has	It's
There is, there was	There's
Are not	Aren't
Is not	Isn't
Will not	Won't

THINK *Write!*

Activity 22.1

Add apostrophes to form contractions. One sentence is correct.

1. I cant believe you ate my leftovers; it wasnt yours to take.
2. Beverly and Lori arent talking to each other, which means Im in the middle.
3. Hes the most selfish person Ive ever met.
4. Her values are similar to mine.
5. Theres a time to celebrate and a time to work; its time to work now.

It's vs. Its

Sometimes the contraction *it's* gives problems because it is confused with the possessive pronoun *its*. Here is a tip to help you not confuse the two words. *It's* is the contraction form of *it is* or *it has*. As you analyze a sentence to determine whether an apostrophe is needed with *its*, mentally put one in and then reread the sentence inserting *it is* or *it has* in place of *its*. If either spelled out form of the contraction makes sense, then you know that you need *it's*. However, if neither spelled out form makes perfect sense, then you know that you need to use *its*.

EXAMPLES

The dog chased its tail.   Insert <u>it is</u> or <u>it has</u>:

> The dog chased <u>it is</u> tail. The dog chased <u>it has</u> tail.

Neither <u>it is</u> nor <u>it has</u> makes sense, so <u>its</u> is correct.

It's hot in here.   Insert <u>it is</u> or <u>it has</u>:

> <u>It is</u> hot in here. <u>It has</u> hot in here.

<u>It is</u> makes sense, so <u>it's</u> is correct.

Note that *its'* is not a word; therefore, it should never be used.

THINK *Write!*

Activity 22.2

Add apostrophes as needed to *its*. Two sentences are correct.

1. Its too bad the Mavericks lost in the first round of the playoffs.
2. The bird fed its young worms.
3. The doctor announced, "Its a boy!"
4. The sore loser whined, "Its just a stupid game; its not really a big deal."
5. The Siamese kitten licked its fur clean.

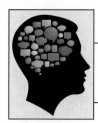

THINK *Write*/TIP

In formal, academic writing, most of your instructors do not allow you to use contractions unless you are writing dialogue or an informal assignment. Check with your instructors regarding their policy concerning contractions.

Singular Possessive

To show ownership or possession of singular nouns or indefinite pronouns, add an apostrophe and an "s."

EXAMPLES

The little boy's bedroom is blue.

Malik's basketball is flat.

Everyone's report is due on Monday.

Sunday's meal consists of steak, mashed potatoes, and string beans.

Last year's annual meeting was held in Orlando.

If the singular word ends in an "s," add an apostrophe and an "s" or just an apostrophe.

EXAMPLE

James's back pack is heavy.

OR

James' back pack is heavy.

THINK *Write!*

Activity 22.3

Add apostrophes as needed to form singular possessives.

1. Toms motorcycle is a Yamaha.
2. The little girls doll can cry, walk, and talk.
3. Wednesdays forecast is for rain.
4. Douglas fathers name is Douglas, also.
5. My friends job is very boring; she works in an antique shop.

Plural Possessive

To show ownership or possession of plural nouns that end in an "s," simply add an apostrophe.

Plural Possessive	Singular Possessive
The players' victory was a surprise to them.	The player's victory was a surprise to her.
The students' essays are due on Thursday.	The student's essay is due on Thursday.
Her parents' motor home is enormous.	Her father's motor home is enormous
The soldiers' guns are shiny.	The soldier's guns are shiny.
The Thompsons' house is blue.	Mr. Thompson's house is blue.
The cities' zoning laws are confusing.	The city's zoning laws are confusing.
I am taking three weeks' vacation in May.	One week's vacation is not long enough.
My two sister-in-laws' houses are large.	My sister-in-law's house is large.

THINK *Write!*

Activity 22.4

Add apostrophes as needed to form plural possessives.

1. The dancers costumes are amazing; they are wearing halos and wings.
2. Their three dogs toys are everywhere.
3. The doctors seminar had to be moved to a larger facility.
4. Seventeen astronauts spacesuits are on display in the science museum.
5. The last two months impromptu jam sessions drew large crowds.

Irregular Plurals

Although most nouns become plural by adding an "s," some words change their spelling when they become plural. For these words, add an apostrophe and an "s" to show ownership or possession.

Singular Possessive		Plural Possessive	Incorrect/Never Use
The child's bike	the child's bikes	The children's bikes	Childrens'
The man's hat	the man's hats	The men's hats	Mens'
The lady's purse	the lady's purses	The ladies' purses	Ladie's
The woman's gun	the woman's guns	The women's guns	Womens'

THINK *Write!*

Activity 22.5

Add apostrophes as needed.

1. The womens club is selling flowers after the program.
2. The mens department is having a sale on suits.
3. The ladies dress shop on Elm St. sells vintage clothing.
4. The childs parents are upset that their daughter did not get the starring role in the childrens play.

Possessive Compound Nouns

Place an apostrophe and "s" ('s) after the second name when two people jointly own something; place an apostrophe and "s" ('s) after each name when they have separate ownership.

Leonardo and Gina's car wash is very successful. (Leonardo and Gina jointly own the car wash.)

Leonardo's and Gina's secretaries are throwing a surprise party for the company. (Leonardo and Gina both have their own secretaries; they do not share one secretary.)

Possessive Pronouns

Do not use an apostrophe with possessive pronouns; they already show ownership. Possessive pronouns include the following: *his, hers, its, mine, ours, theirs,* and *yours.*

Possessive vs. Simply Plural Nouns

Just because a word ends in an "s" does not mean you should automatically add an apostrophe. The word could simply be in its plural form, meaning more than one and not ownership or possession.

EXAMPLE

The sisters are identical twins, so only their parents can tell them apart.

The words *sisters, twins,* and *parents* are simply in their plural form; none of these words are showing possession, so no apostrophes are needed.

THINK Write!

Activity 22.6

Add apostrophes as needed based on all of the apostrophe rules covered so far. Four sentences are correct.

1. The teachers are looking forward to a three-day weekend.
2. Rogers artwork is so powerful, especially his abstract paintings.
3. The twins purchased matching outfits for their fourteenth birthday.
4. The twins parents, Calvin and Melody, are planning a surprise party for them.
5. The party will be at Calvin and Melodys beach house.
6. The parents will get the twins to their party by pretending to take them on individual shopping sprees.
7. One of the twins will ride in her fathers car and the other in her mothers car.
8. The parents and coaches are participating in the fundraiser for the hockey team.
9. The coaches goal is to raise $15,000.
10. One coachs personal goal is to raise $2,000.

Two Common Apostrophe Mistakes: Verbs and Numerals

Do not use apostrophes with any verbs, including ones that end in s.

    Wrong: Lisa want's to win the lottery; she hope's to win soon.

    Correct: Lisa wants to win the lottery; she hopes to win soon.

Also, avoid using apostrophes when writing numerals in general or when writing numerals of a decade or century.

    Wrong: William's 3's look like 5's.   William's three's look like five's.

    Correct: William's 3s look like 5s.   William's threes look like fives.

    Wrong: During the 1970's, disco music was popular.

    Correct: During the 1970s, disco music was popular.

THINK Write!

Activity 22.7

Remove any unneeded apostrophes.

1. Robert enjoy's listening to rap music, which became popular in the 1990's.
2. Julie's parent's constantly ask about her grades; they are proud she brings home 80's and 90's on her assignments.
3. Renee want's to earn a six-figure salary.

Chapter 22 Review Exercise

Insert the fifteen needed apostrophes in the following paragraph.

To Tat or not to Tat

Ricky excitedly walked through the tattoo shops doors. He was eager to get his first tattoo. Ricky planned to get his girlfriends name tattooed over his heart. At first, his parents objected to him getting a tattoo because tattoos are not part of his familys tradition, but Ricky convinced them to let him get one. His fathers main objection was that their two weeks relationship might end before the ink dried while his mothers concern was health related versus relationship related. After reassuring his parents that his feelings for Raelynn were not a mere childs crush but a mans love for a woman and that he would not die from blood poisoning, they consented to let him get his current loves name tattooed permanently on his body. After saving his allowance and his lifeguards salary for a month, Ricky could not believe he was flipping through the tattoo artists book, picking out the lettering for his first tat. Just as the artist was about to put ink on his clients skin, Rickys cell phone rang; he answered and heard his beloveds voice. After a brief one-way conversation, Ricky hung up the phone. Instead of getting Raelynns name tattooed over his heart, Ricky ended up getting a broken heart tattoo in its place.

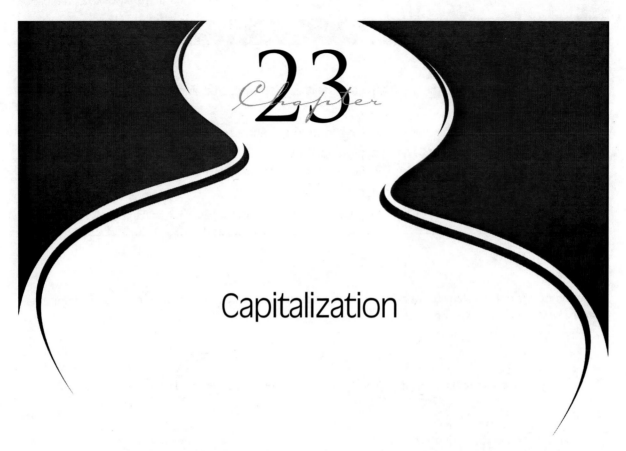

Capitalization

Sometimes you become confused when it comes to capitalization. This chapter covers some of the major and minor rules of capitalization. There are some exceptions that you should be aware of relating to capitalization, and there are also some options that you have when faced with deciding whether a word should or should not be capitalized.

Rule 1

The first letter of proper nouns, such as names of people, specific places, days of the week, holidays, churches, organizations, states, religions, and major historical events, should always be capitalized.

EXAMPLES

President Barack Obama, China, United States of America, Baptist, Eastfield College, New Year's Day

THINK *Write!*

Activity 23.1

Correct the sentences where there are errors in capitalization by capitalizing the needed letters. One sentence is correct.

1. On thanksgiving, our family will depart for a long trip to europe.
2. The game lasted all day Tuesday and finally ended on Wednesday.
3. Mrs. Gulley assigned an essay over the civil war and world war II.
4. After church, we went to a luby's for lunch.
5. The dallas/ft.worth area has grown since the high-five freeway was built.

Rule 2

Common nouns that are general do not require capitalization. A way to determine if a noun is common is to add *a* or *an* in front of the noun. If it makes sense, then it is a common noun.

EXAMPLES

College, a doctor, the seasons (spring, summer, fall, winter), a planet, my spouse, an airplane

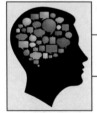 THINK *Write!*/TIP

The word President is always capitalized when referring to the President of the United States of America. For example: The President will attend the inaugural ball.

THINK *Write!*

Activity 23.2

Correct the sentences where there are errors in capitalization. One sentence is correct.

1. Next week Lawyers from SMU will come and lecture to students in the performance hall.
2. Attending Law School is something I have always wanted to do.
3. If you become confused about your schedule, you should ask for help.
4. My Supervisor gave me a raise.
5. During the Fall semester, we will write several essays.

Rule 3

Always capitalize the first word in a sentence, quotation, or items in a list.

EXAMPLES

Not many professors allow students to make up missed assignments.

The student handbook stated: "Disruptions are not allowed anywhere on campus."

The dean reviewed the following criteria:

      Student evaluations

      Student recommendations

      Student concerns

THINK *Write!*

Activity 23.3

Correct the sentences where there are errors in capitalization.

1. the eastfield college library is closed.
2. John F. Kennedy said, "ask not what your country can do for you—ask what you can do for your country."
3. The employer plans to conduct the following before hiring any additional employees:
   - background check
   - credit check
   - reference check

Rule 4

Capitalize the names of directions only if the geographical area is specified.

EXAMPLES

The storm came in from the south.

Stories about the Civil War are in most libraries in the Deep South.

THINK *Write!*

Activity 23.4

Correct the sentences where there are errors in capitalization. Write "C" if any of the sentences are correct.

1. tyson was born in eastern Missouri.
2. When we travel to Oklahoma from Kansas, we will be traveling South.
3. The Midwest is known for having terrible storms.
4. After visiting Southern greece, I gained a better respect for cultural diversity.
5. During the war, the north had a different perception of people who lived in the south.

Rule 5

Capitalize religious names.

EXAMPLES

God, Zeus, Buddha, Mohammad, the Messiah, the Koran, Allah, Baptist

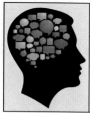

THINK *Write!* / TIP

When referring to "God" as the monotheistic God of Judaism, Christianity, and Islam, capitalize the "G." Additionally, the pronouns referring to God, such as *He*, *Him*, and *His*, must be capitalized. When referring to Greek gods and similar deities, the "g" in god(s) is lowercased.

THINK *Write!*

Activity 23.5

Correct the sentences where there are errors in capitalization.

1. In the movie, zeus was the most powerful god on Mt. Olympus.
2. The Greek god eros, also known by the Roman name of cupid, is the god of love.
3. In World Religion 2301, Shaun is studying christianity, judaism, and islam.
4. Keith attends a catholic church that holds services in both English and Spanish.
5. People who practice hinduism believe the cow is sacred.

Rule 6

Capitalize the first letter of specific time eras and ages.

EXAMPLES

Classical Era, Golden Age, The Harlem Renaissance

THINK *Write!*

Activity 23.6

Correct the sentences where there are errors in capitalization.

1. During the middle ages, many people died of the plague.
2. Many famous authors were introduced during the harlem renaissance period.
3. The victorian era was named for Queen Victoria of England.

Rule 7

Capitalize the pronoun "I."

EXAMPLE

When I go to class, I bring my homework.

THINK *Write!*

Activity 23.7

Correct the sentences where there are errors in capitalization.

1. i enjoy working out and riding horses.
2. When i learned how to drive, i often got speeding tickets.

Rule 8

Capitalize prominent words in titles: the first letter of the first word, only the first letter of major words in the middle, and the first letter of the last word.

EXAMPLES

The Hunger Games

Fast Food Nation

My Three Favorite Holidays

Drowning in Debt

THINK *Write!*

Activity 23.8

Correct the sentences where there are errors in capitalization.

1. *The color Purple* won Best Picture in 1984.
2. I read *Life is So good* on my Kindle.
3. *the secret life of bees* is one of my favorite novels.

Chapter 23 Review Exercise

Capitalize any letters in words that need it. Lowercase any letters in words that should not be capitalized.

Roots to remember

World Renowned Author alex haley wrote several books during his lifetime. Undoubtedly, the novel *roots* is his most controversial novel. The Book focuses on one man's journey to find out where his Family first begins. After several years of research, haley found that his original Roots began in Africa by the gambia River. As he began to piece together his Family tree, he focused on the Patriarch of his Family kunta kinte. Haley begins the story by creating a timeline of how Kunta is captured, sold into Slavery, and brought to the New World. The saga continues when he meets his wife, a slave named bell. Bell and Kunta get married and have a daughter name kizzy. Eventually kizzy grows up, only to be sold out by her master's Niece. Once She is sold, she is determined to become a free Woman. Kizzy gets pregnant by her new Master and has a son name George. George grows up believing that one day he will be free. After years of fighting chickens Overseas for his Master, who is also his father, george finally gains his freedom. Once He receives his Freedom Papers, he sets out on a journey to find his family. The Saga ends when the civil war takes place and all slaves are Freed. This novel still ignites the urge for human and civil rights and is thought to be an unforgettable piece of American History.

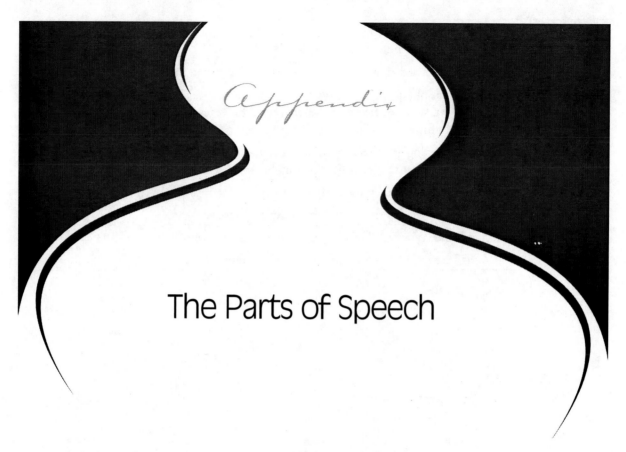

The Parts of Speech

Below are definitions of the parts of speech in the English language. Every part of speech is used in order to help writers and speakers convey meaning in a clear way. Although not all of the parts of speech are used in every sentence, a sentence must contain at least a subject and a verb. Words are classified by their function in a sentence, not their forms. In other words, the word *cook*, for example, can function as a noun in one sentence and as a verb in another.

Articles	*A*, *an*, and *the* come before a noun or a noun phrase in a sentence
	The dog barked.
Nouns	A person, place, thing, or idea
	The *dog* barked all *night* long at the *cat*.
Pronouns	Refer to or take the place of a noun or another pronoun
	The dog owner enjoys walking *her* dog. *She* also enjoys teaching *her* dog tricks.
Adjectives	Describe nouns or pronouns
	The *ferocious* dog growled at the *frightened* mail carrier.
Verbs	Show action or a state of being
	The ferocious dog *growled*. It *was trying* to bite the frightened mail carrier.

(continued)

Adverbs	Describe how an action is being done, or they describe another adjective or adverb (adverbs answer how, when, why, or where)
	The dog growled *very loudly* at the *extremely* frightened mail carrier.
Conjunctions	Join words, phrases, and clauses together in a sentence (FANBOYS: for, and, nor, but, or, yet, so; transitional words: therefore, however; subordinating conjunctions: because, although, if, when)
	Because the dog growled at the mail carrier, she refused to deliver mail to the dog owners' house *or* to their adjacent neighbors' houses.
Prepositions	Part of propositional phrases that contain a noun or pronoun (in, on, at, by, with)
	The dog growled *at* the mail carrier only *on* Tuesdays.
Interjections	Words like Wow! Oh! or Hey! used to express emotion
	Wow! I have never seen a mail carrier run so fast before.

Notes

Common Editing Symbols

Indent your paragraph:

¶ Walmart is a busy place.

Capitalize a letter:

washington was the first president.

De-capitalize a letter:

Many High Schools are overcrowded.

Combine words:

Sam likes to eat ginger bread.

Unclear meaning: ?

Add a comma: ⌄

Add a period: ⊙

Add an apostrophe: ⌄

Spelling: SP

Word choice: WC

Fragment:

Frag
To become a better student. Come to every class meeting.

Comma splice:

C/S
The dog ran wildly out the door, Jerry left it open too long.

Fused sentence:

f/d
The dog ran wildly out the door Jerry left it open too long.

Subject-verb agreement problem:

S-V agreement
Each student in all Mr. Carters classes are passing.

Remove completely:

Sophie sunbathed all morning. She lay in the hammock. ~~The kitchen door was open.~~

Connect to previous paragraph:

    Alex was very sleepy. He took a nap.
    When he awoke, he felt refreshed.

Split the word into two:

Yoroung loves icecream.